SERVING IN
YOUR CHURCH
PRAYER MINISTRY

T0371379

OTHER TITLES IN THE ZONDERVAN PRACTICAL MINISTRY GUIDE SERIES

Paul E. Engle is an executive editor and associate publisher for editorial development at Zondervan. He has served as a pastor and as an instructor in several seminaries. Among the eight books he has written are *Baker's Wedding Handbook, Baker's Funeral Handbook,* and *God's Answers for Life's Needs.*

Charles E. Lawless Jr. is associate professor and senior associate dean of the Billy Graham School of Missions, Evangelism and Church Growth at The Southern Baptist Theological Seminary. He has served as a pastor for almost twenty years. He is the coauthor of *Spiritual Warfare* and the author of *Making Disciples through Mentoring* and *Discipled Warriors.*

ZONDERVAN
PRACTICAL
MINISTRY GUIDES

SERVING IN YOUR CHURCH PRAYER MINISTRY

PAUL E. ENGLE, SERIES EDITOR

CHARLES E. LAWLESS JR.

ZONDERVAN™

GRAND RAPIDS, MICHIGAN 49530 USA

ZONDERVAN™

Serving in Your Church Prayer Ministry
Copyright © 2003 by Charles E. Lawless Jr.

Requests for information should be addressed to:

Zondervan, *Grand Rapids, Michigan 49530*

Library of Congress Cataloging-in-Publication Data

Lawless, Charles E., 1961-
    Serving in your church prayer ministry / Charles E. Lawless, Jr.
      p. cm.
    Includes bibliographical references.
    ISBN 978-0-310-24758-6
    1. Church work. 2. Prayer—Christianity. I. Title.
BV4400 .L39   2003
248.3'2—dc21

                                           2002013589

Interior design by Sherri L. Hoffman

Printed in the United States of America

To the prayer warriors who intercede for
Chuck and his wife, Pam:
Allen and Lisa Lawless, Jim and Ruby Floyd,
Jeff Harvey, Pat Ingram, Frank and Shirley Smith,
Lamont and Vicki Jacobs, Sterling and Karina Gross,
Martin and Norma Hall, and Janet Beck.

CONTENTS

Suppose a young couple moved into your town and started attending your church. Several weeks later you invited them to visit over a cappuccino at the local Starbucks. After some chitchat, you posed the question, "How do you like our church? What one thing stands out most about our church?" How likely is it that the newcomers would answer, "What really impresses us is that you people sure believe in prayer and put it into practice. You seem to be a real prayer-driven church"?

The early church was a prayer-driven church. Why do I say that? Think about Jesus' disciples. They saw him heal the sick, but they didn't ask him to teach them about healing. They listened to him speak like nobody else spoke, but they didn't ask for lessons in public speaking. They watched him minister to all types of people, but they didn't ask for ministry training. Instead, they wanted him to *teach them to pray like he prayed* (Luke 11:1).

They knew that Jesus prayed, and they knew that his prayers made a difference. Is it surprising that these same men—who had learned from the Master how to pray—helped make the early church a praying church?

As you'll see in chapter 1, prayer was at the center of all that the early church did. Now, almost two thousand years later, prayer is still central in growing churches. Growing churches teach prayer and model prayer. In fact, they *expect* their members to pray.

On the other hand, many churches spend more time talking about prayer than they do praying. Leaders know that their churches should be praying (so they encourage members to pray), but they haven't learned how to make prayer a focus of the church.

That's the purpose of this guide—to help you and your church develop an effective prayer ministry and involve everyone who's a part of your church family. As you read through the book, you'll find lots of examples and creative ideas. I hope these will serve not only to motivate you to pray but also to give you practical ideas you can implement in your church.

This guide is designed for group study, although you will surely benefit from reading it on your own. Because a prayer movement in a church usually begins with the few rather than the many, I encourage you to enlist a small group of members (seven to ten persons) who will study this resource with you. You can choose to read the entire book prior to meeting with your group, or you can study each of the seven chapters separately.

Each chapter includes application/evaluation questions within the chapter, as well as discussion questions at the end. While it may be tempting only to *think* about the response, I encourage you to record your thoughts. Writing out the answers will not only facilitate discussion if you are studying with a group, but it will also increase the potential that the information will stick with you throughout this study.

Not all of the questions have one specific required answer. In many cases, the discussion questions allow for a variety of possible responses. Carefully consider your own response, write it down, and then share it with your group.

This book includes reproducible prayer ministry forms. You are welcome to use these forms as part of your ministry. I also encourage you to read the footnotes as you study, and be sure to check out the resources listed in appendix 7 at the end of the book. In both places, you'll find information about other materials and organizations that will help you grow a prayer-driven church.

As your group completes the study, seek God's direction in beginning new groups to study this guide. Ask God to spread the fire of prayer throughout your congregation. My prayer is that your church will become a praying church—and that others will come to your congregation, saying, "Teach us to pray."

ONE

Prayer Matters!

First Church, located in the Midwest, averages about 250 at Sunday morning worship. Several years ago, the church adopted a growth strategy built around six purposes of the church—one of which is prayer.[1] The church wasn't large enough to afford a full-time minister of prayer, so they enlisted a layperson to be the prayer coordinator.

The new prayer leader enthusiastically tackled the challenge. He recruited prayer teams to pray for ministries that supported each of the church's purposes. For example, a team was formed to pray specifically for the church's evangelism and missions efforts. Other teams were formed to pray for the church's fellowship, her worship, and her other central purposes.

The prayer leader also worked with the pastor to provide training opportunities for the members. The pastor preached a series on prayer. At the same time, the church held Sunday evening classes, covering such topics as "How to Pray for Your Unsaved Family Members," "How to Pray for Your Coworkers," and "How to Pray for Your City."

Now the church offers a prayer track in its Wednesday night equipping program, prays weekly for missionaries, and provides multiple opportunities for members to pray together. Under the leadership of the pastor and a committed prayer coordinator, First Church has become a praying church.

---

[1]The other purposes are worship, evangelism, equipping, service, and fellowship. For a more complete discussion, see my book *Discipled Warriors: Arming Your Church for Spiritual Warfare* (Grand Rapids: Kregel, 2002).

One secret behind this church's renewed focus on prayer is simple: *They have a pastor and a prayer leader who believe that prayer matters.* When a church's pastor and leaders really believe that prayer makes a difference, they'll make prayer a priority in their own lives and in the church's life.

The goal of this chapter is to challenge you to raise the level of prayer in your church. The New Testament church serves as the model of a church that prays. Stories of churches that grew as they prayed will encourage you as you strive to become a church "devoted . . . to prayer" (Acts 2:42).

As you begin this study, take time to consider the importance of prayer in your church. Complete activity #1 on the following page, and be prepared to discuss your opinion with other members of your study group. (A suggestion: After you read the following sections on prayer in the early church and in other churches, you may want to do this exercise again.)

THE EARLY CHURCH AND PRAYER

Have you ever thought about how much the early church prayed? Look at these revealing clues from the book of Acts:

- ❏ 1:14 — "They all joined together constantly in prayer."
- ❏ 3:1 — "Peter and John were going up to the temple at the time of prayer."
- ❏ 4:31 — "After they prayed, the place where they were meeting was shaken."
- ❏ 6:4 — "And [we] will give our attention to prayer and the ministry of the word."
- ❏ 10:9 — "Peter went up on the roof to pray."

Activity #1: Rate the priority given to prayer in your church.

Prayer in our church is . . .

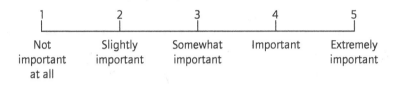

- 12:5 — "The church was earnestly praying to God for him."
- 13:3 — "After they had fasted and prayed, they placed their hands on them and sent them off."
- 14:23 — "Paul and Barnabas . . . with prayer and fasting, committed them to the Lord."
- 16:25 — "Paul and Silas were praying and singing hymns to God."
- 20:36 — "When [Paul] had said this, he knelt down with all of them and prayed."
- 28:8 — "Paul went in to see him and, after prayer, placed his hands on him and healed him."

Clearly, the early church was a praying church. Why? Because they loved Jesus, they were dependent on God, and they knew that prayer made a difference.

The Early Believers Loved Jesus

Because of my teaching and speaking schedule, I'm often out of town and away from my wife. Wherever I am, though, I want to hear her voice and talk with her. Our phone bills are sometimes expensive, but *not* talking to each other isn't an option. We just naturally want to talk with each other, because we're in love.

That's the way it was for many of the early Christians. Though they needed direction in how to pray (Ephesians 6:18–20; Colossians 4:2; 1 Thessalonians 5:17; James 5:13–16), talking with God was as natural for them as a wife talking to her husband or a son talking to his father (Romans 8:15–17). Jesus' love for them had motivated him to teach them to pray, and their love for him motivated them to follow him in prayer.

In reality, however, we sometimes get so busy "doing church" that we neglect our love relationship with God. Our church activities continue (often in abundance), but we give too little attention to our personal spiritual walk. Driven by duty rather than by love for God, we work harder in church but often pray less.

A church that wants to be a prayer-driven church will first make sure that she has kept her "first love," that is, that her

---

Activity #2: Mark the statement(s) below that you believe most accurately describe(s) your church:

_____1. As a whole, our church loves God more now than we ever have; because we love him, we strive to obey him.

_____2. Our church probably loved God more in years past than we do now.

_____3. Our church is learning to love God again.

_____4. We have a lot of church activities, but we don't talk much about simply loving God and obeying him.

_____5. We probably need to rekindle our love for God if we want to become a praying church.

---

members love God more than they ever have (Revelation 2:4). If they really love Jesus, they will keep his commandments (John 14:15).

The Early Believers Were Dependent on God

Genuine prayer indicates not only love but also dependence. The prayers of the early believers showed that they were dependent on God for food (Matthew 6:11), health (James 5:13–16), power (Acts 1:8, 14), protection (Matthew 6:13), and guidance (Acts 1:24–25). They also knew that only God could grow the church (1 Corinthians 3:6–7).

The early church recognized that they couldn't face a tough world without God's directing them. In fact, the apostle Paul himself needed prayer support to be a bold witness for God (Ephesians 6:19–20). His call was dramatic (Acts 9:1–19) and his commitment was sure (2 Timothy 4:7–8), but even Paul needed God's daily strength to fulfill his mission.

I recently led a group of American Christians on a mission trip to Moscow, Russia, to teach the Russian believers about prayer. At our first meeting, the Russians stood to pray (as they always do) and then led us in a two-hour prayer meeting. Throughout the next two weeks, the Russian brothers and sisters taught *us* more about prayer than we could ever have taught them.

They typically prayed for hours, with hearts broken over unbelieving family members and friends. They interceded passionately, believing that God would be faithful to hear their prayers. These believers—whose faith had often cost them dearly—had learned through hardship to trust God. In the end, their dependence affected the way they prayed.

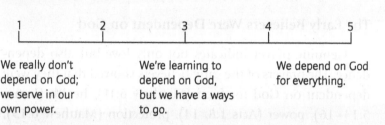

Activity #3: Evaluate your church's dependence on God, using the scale below.

Prayer-driven churches are churches that depend on God. On the other hand, churches that operate in their own power usually don't pray much.

The Early Believers Knew Prayer Made a Difference

Many of the early believers were Jews who had converted to Christianity. Very likely they knew from their Scriptures many stories about the power of prayer.

Abraham interceded for the cities of Sodom and Gomorrah, and Lot was rescued (Genesis 18:20–33; 19:29). Moses prayed for water, and God provided it (Exodus 15:22–25). Hannah prayed for a son, whom God gave her (1 Samuel 1:1–20). Solomon gained his wisdom through prayer (1 Kings 3:1–15). Elijah prayed on Mount Carmel, and the God of Israel revealed his authority over the prophets of Baal (1 Kings 18:36–39). Nehemiah sought his king's favor through prayer, and God granted that favor (Nehemiah 1:4–2:8). Daniel's commitment to prayer landed him in the lions' den, but God protected him there (Daniel 6:1–28).

Try putting yourself in the place of a typical member of the early church. It's very likely that you had learned the stories of effective prayer in the Old Testament. Or maybe you had seen Jesus pray and knew that his prayers were powerful (Luke 11:1). Likely you had seen God answer your own prayers, as well as those of other brothers and sisters. Though members of your church were sometimes still surprised by God's answers (see Acts 12:1-17), you knew that "the prayer of a righteous man is powerful and effective" (James 5:16). Is it any wonder that members of the early church prayed as much as they did? When we really believe that prayer makes a difference, we'll pray more.

Step back into your church once again and evaluate your congregation's belief in the power of prayer.

A TALE OF TWO CHURCHES

In most cases, our churches don't match the early church's commitment to prayer. The challenge is usually great if we want

Activity #4: Mark the statement(s) below that best describe(s) how you see your church.

_____ 1. We talk about prayer, but I'm not sure we really believe that prayer is effective.

_____ 2. Without question, we believe that prayer makes a difference.

_____ 3. We say we believe that prayer makes a difference, but we still pray too little.

_____ 4. Our church turns to prayer before we do anything else.

_____ 5. We don't give enough attention to praising God for answered prayer.

to grow a church that really prays. So listen now to the stories of two praying churches in London and New York. May they inspire you as you, your church leaders, and your fellow members tackle this challenge.

Tabernacle #1

Their young pastor was only twenty years old when he began to serve this London church as pastor. The membership numbered 232, and the crowd has been estimated between 80 and 200 on those first Sundays. During the next thirty-eight years of the pastor's ministry, over 14,000 people joined the church. The congregation at times exceeded 10,000, and the pastor occasionally asked church members to stay home in order that newcomers might have a seat.

Maybe you recognize this church as the Metropolitan Tabernacle (originally the New Park Street Chapel), pastored by Charles Spurgeon from 1854 to 1892. Spurgeon himself was a man of great prayer, and he led the church to build a great prayer ministry.

Every Monday night, church members gathered at a church-wide prayer meeting that Spurgeon called the "council of war." Travelers from abroad and members from other churches often joined in the prayer meeting. For many, this meeting was *the* gathering of the week in a church committed to prayer, a church led by a pastor consumed by prayer.

Listen to how Spurgeon described these prayer meetings:

We began this work with a little handful of Christian men. I remember the first Monday night after I came to London; there was a slender audience on the Sabbath, but thank God there was almost as many at the prayer-meeting as on Sunday; and I thought, "This is all right; these people can pray." They did pray, and as we increased in prayer we increased in numbers. Sometimes at prayer-meetings, my heart was almost ready to break for joy because of the mighty supplication that was offered.[2]

In addition to praying on Monday nights, groups of believers prayed daily at Metropolitan Tabernacle. The pastor, deacons, and elders gathered to pray prior to the Sunday morning service. Special prayer meetings to support the church's evangelistic and Sunday school efforts were common. Prayer was, in the words of her pastor, "the steam engine which makes the wheels revolve."[3]

Tabernacle #2

Over a century after Charles Spurgeon became the pastor of Metropolitan Tabernacle, another minister in his late twenties became pastor of an inner-city church in New York. The church met in a run-down building, and the congregation numbered fewer than thirty.

The young pastor found the challenges of the ministry overwhelming. A lack of church funds forced the pastor and his wife to take second jobs to pay their bills. The problems of the inner city were enormous, including drug and alcohol addiction, disintegrating families, and destructive lifestyles.

---

[2] Charles Haddon Spurgeon, "The Special Prayer Meeting," in *The Metropolitan Tabernacle Pulpit*, vol. 21 (Pasadena, Calif.: Pilgrim Publications, 1971), 443.

[3] Spurgeon, "The Special Prayer Meeting," 437.

Facing these difficulties, the pastor sensed God's call to him to lead his church to prayer. He did so by echoing the words of Spurgeon, challenging his congregation to make prayer "the engine that will drive the church."[4] Almost thirty years later—in 2002—an average of over six thousand people attend the church.

You may know this church as Brooklyn Tabernacle, pastored by Jim Cymbala. Probably best known for its choir, the church is also noted for its prayer ministry. A Tuesday night prayer meeting with an average weekly attendance of two thousand anchors this ministry. Visitors from around the world often attend.

In addition to the weekly prayer meeting, Brooklyn Tabernacle sponsors the "Prayer Band," a twenty-four-hour intercessory prayer ministry. Teams of prayer warriors pray in all-night prayer meetings. Prayer teams intercede for the pastor and congregation during worship services, intensifying their prayers during the altar call. Teams also prayerfully support the evangelistic outreach events of the church.

Brooklyn Tabernacle, as well as Metropolitan Tabernacle under Spurgeon's leadership, are models of praying churches. In fact, both are examples of churches that were small but *grew as they prayed—and prayed as they grew*. Their examples challenge us to grow churches that are truly houses of prayer (Matthew 21:13).

CONCLUSION

So where do you begin if you want to grow a prayer-driven church? From the opening story of this chapter to the examples

---

[4]Jim Cymbala, *Fresh Wind, Fresh Fire: What Happens When God's Spirit Invades the Heart of His People* (Grand Rapids: Zondervan, 1997), 27.

of the two churches, you should have noticed similar charac-
teristics among churches that have effective prayer ministries.

Praying churches have praying pastors. Praying churches
have praying leaders. Praying churches make prayer a priority.
Above all, prayer-driven churches believe that prayer matters.
They understand that prayer is a reflection of their relationship
with God; they pray because they love Jesus. They recognize
their dependence on God, knowing that the triune God is the
head of the church (Ephesians 5:23–24). And they know from
the Bible and from their own experience that prayer really does
make a difference.

To begin leading your church to be a prayer-driven church,
ask God to teach you and your study group to pray. Agree to
become a praying church, perhaps using a covenant similar to
the sample below. Believe together that prayer really *does* matter!

Prayer Group Covenant

Believing that prayer is essential to our church, I, _____,
commit myself to the study of *Serving in Your Church Prayer Ministry*.
I am committed to

- completing my assignments and attending all scheduled training sessions.
- seeking daily to love Jesus and depend on him.
- asking God daily to teach our church to pray.
- praying daily for my pastor, church leaders, and group members.
- praising God for answered prayers and, as opportunities arise,
  encouraging others with these stories.

_____   _____
Participant   Date

QUESTIONS FOR REFLECTION AND DISCUSSION

1. Using the exercises in this chapter, evaluate the overall spiritual condition of your church. What can you do as an individual to improve your church's prayer life? What can be done to address any weaknesses?

2. Study the prayer life of Jesus by reading the references in Luke's gospel (Luke 3:21–22; 5:15–16; 6:12; 9:18, 28–29; 10:21–22; 11:1; 23:46). What are some of the key insights you learn about prayer?

3. Becoming a praying church usually requires change. What do you think will be required in order for your church to become a praying church? What will be required of you?

4. As a group, pray for your pastor and church leaders. Pray also that all church leaders and members, beginning with you, will capture the vision of being a praying church.

TWO

Organizing for Prayer

H ave you heard about the incredible prayer movement taking place in Korean churches? Many Korean churches open their doors at 5:00 A.M. every day for prayer. Some hold prayer retreats on "prayer mountains." Korean pastors often pray for several hours a day.

Suwon Brothers Church in Suwon, South Korea, is one of these praying churches where dawn prayer meetings take place each day. Church leaders teach a "prayer school" each Friday. A monthly prayer calendar lists ten to fifteen specific prayer requests for each day. Wednesday worship services focus on praying for unreached people groups around the world. Elderly members of the church hold their own prayer meetings. Members are taught to pray for nonbelievers during their devotions.[1]

Prayer permeates all that Suwon Brothers Church does. What do you think it takes to develop this kind of prayer-driven church? As we learned in chapter 1, praying leaders are essential. Yet, many leaders and church members who are fervent prayer warriors struggle to maintain a strong prayer ministry in their churches. A passion for God and for prayer must be combined with effective organization if you want your church to become a prayer-driven church.

---

[1]I am deeply indebted to my Korean doctoral students for providing this information.

TAKING THE FIRST STEPS

Americans will never forget the tragic events of September 11, 2001. The hijacked planes crashing into the World Trade Center towers and the Pentagon shook our world, and the cries for retaliation were swift and loud. We wanted immediate justice.

Quite a bit of time passed, though, before our military forces took action to root out the terrorists in Afghanistan. Why did it take so long? Though the reasons are complex, one basic reason was that an effective response demanded organization. Disorganized military power can quickly lose its effectiveness.

That's the way a prayer ministry operates, too. A church has the power of prayer at her fingertips, but a disorganized, unfocused prayer ministry is usually ineffective. Here are five simple steps for getting a prayer ministry started in your church.

Start with the Few—Build a Core Group of Prayer Warriors

The best place to begin a prayer ministry is on your knees. Ask God to direct you to other church members who will join you in praying for your church to become a praying church. Then come together and simply pray for God's direction for this potential ministry.

In some ways, this first step may seem odd to you. You may be asking such questions as, "Can't we just get a canned program and begin a prayer movement in our church?" or "Do we really need to pray about *a prayer ministry?*"

Here's the reason for this first step: A prayer ministry is hard work, and Satan will do all he can to oppose your church's efforts to become a prayer-driven church. Church staff members may not be demonstrably supportive. Some members may not want to serve in a behind-the-scenes ministry such as prayer. Discouragement will sometimes affect even the staunchest prayer warriors. In light of the spiritual battles surrounding a prayer ministry, doesn't it make sense to pray with a core group even before you begin the ministry?

If the Pastor Isn't Already on Board, Secure His Support

Our research teams at the Billy Graham School of Missions, Evangelism and Church Growth have studied thousands of growing churches since 1995. In almost every study conducted, we've seen two recurrent themes: (1) Prayer is essential to reaching nonbelievers, and (2) a praying pastor is essential to a powerful prayer ministry.[2] One California prayer warrior even told us that when she started praying for her nonsupportive pastor, God moved him out and brought in another shepherd who enthusiastically supported the prayer ministry![3]

Diana Klungel is a ministry associate and prayer ministry leader at Calvary Christian Reformed Church in Holland, Michigan. Her church is a praying church that has identified and trained intercessors, established prayer support for staff members, and used short-term prayer projects (for example, Fifty Days of Prayer) to involve their congregation in prayer. Listen to Diana describe what she's learned about a prayer ministry: "Most valuable to me [as I work with prayer ministry here] is a senior pastor who really encourages and mobilizes and preaches

---

[2]See, for example, Thom S. Rainer, *Effective Evangelistic Churches* (Nashville: Broadman & Holman, 1995); Rainer, *High Expectations* (Nashville: Broadman & Holman, 1998).

[3]Rainer, *Effective Evangelistic Churches*, 72.

[and obviously models] the value of prayer. It is essential."[4] Simply stated, a church's prayer ministry will seldom be effective without the pastor's visible and genuine support.

Ideally, your pastor will have a heart for prayer and will be one of the leaders in the core group already praying. If he isn't on board, though, lead the group to pray for his support. (And don't give up easily—most pastors want their churches praying, though not all understand the importance of a corporate prayer ministry.)

Ask God to give your pastor . . .

❏ a heart that is more passionate for prayer than ever before.

❏ a vision of what might happen in the church and community if the members really started praying.

❏ a desire to lead the church toward becoming a praying church through modeling prayer, preaching and teaching about prayer, and equipping members to pray.

❏ a clear understanding that you and others are willing to start and maintain this ministry so that the pastor won't be overwhelmed with yet another responsibility.

Activity #1: Write out a one-sentence prayer that you can use to pray for your pastor *each day* during the time you are studying this book.

Enlist a Prayer Ministry Coordinator

Though the title differs from church to church (for example, prayer director, minister of prayer, prayer leader, prayer

---

[4]Personal correspondence with Brett Champion, research assistant.

coordinator), most congregations with effective prayer ministries have one member who oversees the ministry. In some cases, this is a paid staff position, but in most cases the leader is a volunteer layperson. This sample job description may give you direction as you seek this important leader:

Job Description for a Prayer Coordinator

Qualifications:

1. Must be a faithful Christian and church member
2. Must exhibit a strong spiritual life and an obvious passion for prayer
3. Must possess leadership skills and be respected in the congregation
4. Must have a teachable, humble spirit

Responsibilities:

1. Help ensure that prayer is integrated into every ministry of the church
2. Enlist and oversee a prayer committee or team
3. Plan and organize special prayer emphases in the church
4. Coordinate regularly scheduled prayer training events
5. Promote the prayer ministry
6. Oversee calendar and budget items related to the prayer ministry
7. Serve as church liaison with prayer leaders from other churches
8. Whenever feasible, attend prayer leader training events

For many years, Mrs. Nell Bruce was the prayer coordinator for Highview Baptist Church in Louisville, Kentucky. My first encounter with Nell took place at the conclusion of a Sunday morning service. My wife and I met her in the aisle of the church as the crowd was heading toward the parking lot.

I introduced myself as a new seminary professor, to which Nell quickly responded, "Good to meet you. Let's pray." There, in the middle of several hundred people trying to get to Sunday lunch, Nell prayed for our home, our ministry, our families, and our outreach efforts. She even prayed for our prayer lives, challenging us through prayer to be more committed to intercession. Now that's the kind of prayer coordinator every prayer-driven church needs!

Activity #2: After reviewing the job description for a prayer coordinator, list names of church members you think could serve in this position in your church. Don't forget to consider yourself—God may want you to oversee this ministry.

_____   _____

_____   _____

_____   _____

Establish a Set Direction for the Ministry

The pastor, prayer coordinator, and other appropriate church leaders should work together to develop a purpose statement and general goals for the prayer ministry. For those (like myself) who would rather jump into action than get bogged down in concepts, remember that clear purposes and goals provide direction as well as a means for evaluation.

Ask your pastor to preach about the purpose of prayer in your church. Then work to adopt a simple purpose statement for the prayer ministry that can be easily memorized. Include the statement on any correspondence about the prayer ministry. Publish it in the church newsletter. Consider providing T-shirts for members involved in the ministry. Your goal is to make it almost impossible for regular attenders *not* to know about the church's commitment to prayer. Plan to review the statement and goals at least annually, making sure that everyone involved in the ministry is heading in the same direction.

These sample purpose statements and goals can give you some guidance in this process:

Church A: The purpose of the prayer ministry of _____ Church is to glorify God by equipping believers to relate to God through prayer.

Goals:

1. We will provide semiannual training events.
2. We will seek to provide prayer training for new believers as soon as possible following their baptism.

Church B: The prayer ministry of _____ Church exists to promote individual, local church, and citywide praying that pleases God and breaks the Enemy's strongholds.

Goals:

1. To involve at least 25 percent of our members in prayer training each year
2. To provide citywide prayer training at least once a year
3. To promote Christian unity and prayer in the city
4. To train prayer leaders who focus on specific ministries of the church (men's ministry, student ministry, and so forth)

Enlist a Prayer Leadership Team

Under the direction of the prayer coordinator, enlist a prayer leadership team (called a "committee" in some churches) that will work alongside the coordinator. Use the adopted purpose statement to make sure that team members are on board with the ministry's direction.

The size of the team will vary according to the size of the church, though I've seldom seen an effective prayer leadership team with more than seven to ten members. In a small church,

---

Activity #3: Evaluate the prayer ministry of your church by responding to each of the following questions:

1. Does your church have an active prayer ministry with a recognized prayer leader? _____

2. In your opinion, what percentage of active church members pray daily? _____

3. How often does the pastor preach specifically about prayer? _____
_____

4. Does your church offer prayer training at least once a year? _____
_____

5. Assume that your church has a weekly prayer meeting for all members. What percentage of active members would likely attend?____
_____

6. Does the church budget include funds for developing the prayer ministry? _____

7. At this point, which of the following words best describe your church's prayer ministry? Circle all the words you think are accurate.

   nonexistent   losing ground   alive, but comatose
   weak, but growing   in revival   organized and powerful

Appendix 1 includes a personal prayer survey that can also help you evaluate prayer in your church. I encourage you to get feedback from at least 25 percent of your active members. This information is so important that you may want to take some time during a worship service to have members complete the survey.

the team may be only a few people who help facilitate most activities related to prayer. Team members in a large church are typically responsible for only one component of the prayer ministry, such as the prayer room, special prayer events, neighborhood praying, or evangelistic praying—things I'll talk about later in the book.

The prayer coordinator is usually the best person to recruit team members, and the best people to be recruited are those who already have a heart for particular ministries. A committed small group member, for example, will likely pray more passionately for that ministry. As much as possible, build your team around burdens God has already laid on your church members' hearts.

Take a moment now to review these important steps toward organizing an effective prayer ministry:

- ❑ Build a core group of prayer warriors.
- ❑ Secure the pastor's support.
- ❑ Enlist a prayer ministry coordinator.
- ❑ Establish a set direction for the ministry.
- ❑ Enlist a prayer leadership team.

Having done all these steps, now pray on!

MOVING FORWARD

The building committee of First Community Church was trying to finalize an estimate for a proposed new worship center. To their surprise, the builder said his estimate could change once his crews began to dig the basement of the new structure. "Everything depends on what we find in the ground," he said.

"If we find rock, there could be significant additional cost to blast it away. You just don't know for sure until you know more precisely what you're trying to build on."

That same principle applies to building a prayer ministry: You need to know first what you're building on in order to develop a strong ministry. For that reason, one of the first tasks of the prayer coordinator and prayer leadership team is to assess the current state of prayer in the church.

Once your prayer coordinator and team members have evaluated your church's prayer ministry, the next step is to begin addressing the issues raised. You might discover, for example, that many of your members haven't been taught how to pray; if so, offering more training would be a logical step. Or the survey might reveal that some members just aren't convinced that prayer works. Prayer testimonies in the worship services are one way to change this perception.

The rest of this book will offer suggestions for leading your church to become a prayer-driven church. For now, simply remember that disorganization will get in the way of reaching this goal. As you continue reading and studying with your group, keep in mind the specific issues in your church's prayer ministry that need to be addressed.

CONCLUSION

Have you ever built a home? If so, you've probably been amazed by the organized efforts that change a blueprint into a house. Somehow a drawing becomes a very real residence where you eat, sleep, and live.

That's my goal in this chapter—to help you move from a "drawing" of a prayer ministry to a real "house of prayer" ministry that changes lives. A strong, clear organizational structure will help your church get there.

QUESTIONS FOR REFLECTION AND DISCUSSION

1. Who in your church is currently most responsible for promoting prayer? How often do you pray for this leader?

2. What do you think are the primary obstacles to an effective prayer ministry in your church? How would you address these obstacles?

3. What is *your* vision for your church's prayer ministry? If you were given permission to set two goals for this ministry to accomplish over the next year, what would they be?

4. Are you willing to serve as a member of your church's prayer leadership team? Why or why not?

THREE

Prioritizing Prayer in Your Church

I n November 2001, more than 275 men gathered at the New
Life Church in Colorado Springs, Colorado, in response to a
"Call to War" proclaimed by Bill McCartney of Promise Keepers. Evangelicals, charismatics, and mainline Christians came
together to reclaim their responsibility to be prayer warriors on
behalf of their families, their churches, and their nation. These
men engaged the battle on their knees.[1]

Prayer-driven churches realize that we are wrestling against
principalities and powers (Ephesians 6:12) and that prayer is
not an optional weapon in this battle. Urgent, persistent prayer
is a priority in a praying church.

SETTING THE AGENDA

Calvin Johnson, founding pastor of Solid Rock Christian
Church in Colorado Springs, Colorado, established his church
on prayer. He spends at least one hour each day in prayer. His
church staff includes a prayer leader, who has served in that role
since 1999. Yet listen to the pastor's words: "The greatest challenge to prayer in our church is keeping people interested. They
don't see the value and importance of prayer, or they forget it."[2]

---

[1] "Call to War," *Connected: The Bimonthly Newsletter of the National Association of Local Church Prayer Leaders* (December 2001): 1–3.

[2] "Pastor Profile," *Connected: The Bimonthly Newsletter of the National
Association of Local Church Prayer Leaders* (February 2002): 3.

Even pastors with a passion for prayer must work hard to keep their church focused on prayer. Pastors, prayer coordinators, and other church leaders need to work together to prioritize prayer if a church wants to be a prayer-driven church.

STAFFING FOR PRAYER

If you're familiar with the National Association of Local Church Prayer Leaders, you'll know it as an organization that helps prayer leaders "initiate, strengthen, and expand the prayer ministries of the congregation."[3] The NALCPL recognizes that one way to prioritize prayer in a church is to enlist or hire a specific person to lead the ministry.

Our research at the Billy Graham School also validates the importance of having an official prayer leader. Most effective evangelistic churches have a churchwide prayer ministry, led by a staff member or a designated layperson who has a burden for prayer. In most cases, the laypersons are women. Typically, these prayer leaders have a burning passion for prayer that encourages others to become intercessors.

Twyla Fagan is one of these prayer leaders. Twyla works with a Hispanic congregation in Kentucky whose commitment to prayer is evident in their purpose statement: "Prayer, Love, and Obedience." In addition to weekly congregational prayer meetings, the church holds women's prayer retreats, prayer vigils, and prayer training events. The church also spent four months studying prayer in Sunday school classes.

---

[3]NALCPL Website (www.nalcpl.net). I encourage prayer leaders to join this organization. Its support and resources can be invaluable to a church's prayer ministry.

Prayer-driven churches enlist persons like Twyla as prayer leaders and then publicly support them within the congregation. Some churches commission their prayer leaders in a special service similar to a pastor or elder/deacon ordination service. This kind of service—especially when led by the senior pastor and supported by other leaders—says to the church, "This ministry is a priority for us."

CALENDARING FOR PRAYER

I have the privilege of participating in local church consultations alongside Thom Rainer, one of America's foremost consultants and experts in the field of church growth. Dr. Rainer always looks at the church's calendar and budget as an important way of determining a church's priorities. You can usually tell the heart of a church by knowing what activities they plan and how they spend their money.

A quick glance at the yearly calendar of one prayer-driven church (see pages 40–41) will show that prayer really matters in this church. You'll also see one reason why the pastor and prayer leader are so important to the prayer ministry. If the pastor doesn't support the ministry, a church likely won't have an open door to plan this many prayer events. What's more, no pastor can lead this many events—a good prayer leader will oversee the entire ministry and assume this responsibility on his behalf.

Activity #1: Think about the activities on your church calendar for the next few months. On the basis of the calendar, how important is prayer in your church?

_____ Very important   _____ Somewhat important
_____ Not very important   _____ Not important at all

Yearly Prayer Calendar

REGULAR PRAYER ACTIVITIES EACH MONTH

- daily prayer room intercession
- weekly prayer meetings
- monthly women's prayer meeting
- monthly men's prayer meeting
- monthly senior adult prayer meeting
- prayer training during new members' class
- monthly pastor's prayer partner meeting
- quarterly prayer breakfasts

SPECIAL EVENT(S)

JANUARY

- watch night prayer service (New Year's Eve into New Year's Day)
- public commitment service to pray daily during the next year

FEBRUARY

- prayer service for marriages (around Valentine's Day)
- one-day prayer training event

MARCH

- prayer revival, led by a well-known speaker on prayer

APRIL

- four-week prayer training study, built on prayer revival
- prayer service for North American missionaries

MAY

- prayer service for families
- one-day training: "How to Pray for Your Children"

JUNE

- prayer service for Vacation Bible School workers

JULY

- election of new prayer team members
- enlistment of prayer room volunteers

AUGUST

- prayer service for church workers who begin their positions in the fall

SEPTEMBER

- youth training: "How to Pray for Your Friends"
- deacons' training: "Praying for Church Families"

OCTOBER

- prayer service for the pastor and his family (led by the deacons) during Pastor Appreciation Month
- training for Sunday school prayer leaders

NOVEMBER

- prayer service for the persecuted church
- annual Thanksgiving prayer service

DECEMBER

- prayer service for international missionaries
- annual recognition dinner for prayer ministry volunteers

BUDGETING FOR PRAYER

Of course, plans seldom get accomplished if no money is available to support the plans. Prayer-driven churches plan prayer events, and they make sure that the budget reflects this commitment. A budget for the prayer ministry might include everything from staff salaries to prayer room furniture to photocopies (see the sample budget provided in appendix 2). If your church has limited funds, the budget may contain only such essential items as prayer request forms and mailing costs. In any case, intentional budgeting for prayer ministry gives the ministry significance.

Activity #2: Take a look at your current church budget. On the basis of the budget, how important is prayer in your church?

_____ Very important   _____ Somewhat important
_____ Not very important   _____ Not important at all

PROVIDING SPACE FOR PRAYER: PRAYER ROOMS

As a young Christian, I wasn't sure what to think when I heard the term *prayer room.* My first assumption was that the place was always very quiet. My second assumption was that only old people go there. Essentially, I thought a prayer room was like a hospital chapel where you go only when you're facing an emergency. Now, many years later, I see a prayer room as a place of action — almost like a war room where the troops get their orders and renew their strength.

While not all prayer-driven churches have a prayer room, to have a place set aside only for prayer does suggest that prayer is a priority in a church. If your church is considering a prayer room, be sure to ask several questions in preparation:

❑ Will the room be a new room (an addition) or the renovation of an existing room? Most churches use an existing room, unless they are in the middle of a building program. Accessibility and visibility are important issues when choosing a room, although I've seen well-utilized prayer rooms in closets, storage spaces, under steps, and even in a church bus!

❏ Will there be an outside entrance with security lighting for people who want to pray when the church is locked? Will entrance require a password or code?

❏ Will the prayer room have a telephone and answering machine to receive prayer requests? Will Internet/e-mail access be available?

❏ Who will be responsible for the room? Who will lock and unlock the door? Who will keep the room clean?

Some prayer rooms are small, simple rooms with only a desk, a chair, and a card file that contains the prayer concerns. Others are more elaborate, with several prayer stations in a large room. For instance, members pray for the staff at one station, missionaries at another, the sick at a third station, nonbelievers at the fourth, and all other concerns at a fifth station. Appendix 3 provides an illustration of this type of prayer room (see page 101).

At a minimum, a prayer room should include a desk and chairs, a bulletin board or marker board for messages and prayer concerns, a bookshelf for supplies, and a clock. Optional furnishings include a world map, a kneeling bench, a coatrack, a CD or cassette player, and a storage cabinet.

Two issues are critical if your church wants to develop an effective prayer room. First, you must have a plan to recruit and train prayer volunteers. I'll deal more with this important topic in chapter 6, where I'll talk about reproducing prayer warriors. Second, a clear, well-publicized process for securing, praying for, and updating concerns must also be in place. The process varies in each church, but this chapter will give you some general guidelines for developing your church's method.

Prayer requests may given in at least five ways:

❏ prayer request cards placed in the offering plate during a worship service (see appendix 4 for a card sample)
❏ prayer request cards placed in designated collection spots around the church building, such as well-designed boxes at several entrances
❏ prayer requests phoned in to a particular phone number or designated church member, and then transferred to the appropriate form
❏ prayer requests sent by means of an e-mail message to a designated church member, who then transfers the information to the appropriate form
❏ prayer requests given to designated prayer leaders in small groups, who then send the information to leaders of the prayer room ministry

Requests may be categorized in the prayer room according to the type of need. One church sorts prayer requests into file card holders labeled "urgent requests," "health concerns," "job and financial concerns," "family concerns," and "salvation concerns." In addition, they provide a prayer notebook that includes names and pictures of all church members and staff members. One of the most important places in this prayer room is the white board, where answered prayers are noted daily.

Prayer volunteers should also have an established pattern for praying for the concerns. Some churches expect intercessors to spend five to ten minutes at each station, praying for as many listed concerns as possible in the available time. They

Activity #3: Which of these statements best reflects your church's prayer room?

____ There is no prayer room.
____ We have a prayer room, but it is not effectively used.
____ We're making progress in the way the prayer room is used, but there's still room for improvement.
____ Our prayer room is used often, and it is organized effectively.

then mark their ending point on the list, where another intercessor will begin. Other congregations ask intercessors to pray for only one type of need each week. For example, Judy may pray this week for health needs, while Peter may focus only on the church staff. Next week, their responsibilities may be reversed. Still other churches invite prayer warriors to pray simply as the Lord leads them.

Finally, an effective follow-up plan must be in place. Always encourage those who make prayer requests to provide updates. Enlist a "follow-up" volunteer who calls or sends an e-mail message to get the information. Occasionally place announcements in the church bulletin or newsletter, reminding members to update the information with regard to their prayer requests. Make sure the church knows about *answered* prayers. Doing so will inspire your intercessors to pray on, and it will encourage others to join the prayer team as well.

PUBLICIZING PRAYER

My colleague Mark Terry has written a kind of "tool kit" for pastors called *Church Evangelism.* In his chapter on reaching the community through media, Mark makes this simple but profound statement: "Here is the basic principle of church advertising: *People can only come to your church if they know it exists.*"[4] I would change only a few words and say the same thing about a prayer ministry: People in your church and community can support and utilize your ministry only if they know it exists. Prayer-driven churches let people know that prayer matters to them.

Opportunities for promoting the prayer ministry in the church are numerous:

- ❑ Enlist representatives in each of the church's small groups to keep others informed about the ministry.
- ❑ Write articles for the church newsletter and bulletin.
- ❑ Establish an e-mail "prayergram" to send to members.
- ❑ Have intercessors give testimonies during the worship services.
- ❑ Preach about prayer.
- ❑ Ask children to create pictures and posters describing the importance of prayer.
- ❑ Produce a brief video about this ministry.
- ❑ Annually set up a "prayer ministry booth" for a couple of Sundays.
- ❑ Include a prayer skit in a Sunday morning service.
- ❑ Introduce the ministry and its leaders in church membership classes.

At the same time you're promoting prayer in the church, the community also needs to know about your prayer ministry. Your congregation should get the word out that prayer is a pri-

---

[4]John Mark Terry, *Church Evangelism* (Nashville: Broadman & Holman, 1997), 163.

ority in your church. Here are some ways to publicize the prayer ministry in the community:

- ❏ Place a prayer line phone number or e-mail address in local newspapers.
- ❏ Make sure the church's ad in the Yellow Pages includes prayer information.
- ❏ Do announcements on Christian and secular radio stations.
- ❏ Develop a Website about the ministry.
- ❏ Rent a billboard.
- ❏ Give prayer ministry "business cards" to area chaplains to distribute to hurting people.
- ❏ Ask local newspaper editors to feature a story about the ministry.
- ❏ Send flyers to community residents through direct mail.
- ❏ Seek permission to distribute flyers in parking lots of local restaurants and shopping malls.

CONCLUSION

Valley View Church in Louisville, Kentucky, has a unique plan to show that prayer is important to them. They've received permission from several area business owners to place "prayer request boxes" at these businesses. Customers write out prayer concerns, members from Valley View collect them and pray over the needs, and others follow up if possible with the people who submitted the requests.

Members and community alike are learning that Pastor Kevin Hamm is leading a church for whom prayer is a priority. May God help your church to make prayer a priority, too.

QUESTIONS FOR REFLECTION AND DISCUSSION

1. Is prayer a priority in your life? Is it a priority in the life of your church?

2. What changes might your church want to make in its scheduling and budgeting so that prayer is more obviously made a priority?

3. Are you willing to volunteer for the church's prayer room, if and when you have one? Why or why not?

4. What can you do to help your church publicize her commitment to prayer?

FOUR

Praying for Leaders

J ohn Guernsey is the pastor of All Saints Episcopal Church, a growing church in Woodbridge, Virginia. Members serve in the prayer room ministry for more than 168 hours per week. The prayer room includes a station where members pray specifically for the church's pastoral leaders.

Pastor Guernsey and his associate use a cassette recorder to record their personal prayer requests each week. Prayer room participants listen to these concerns and then intercede for their leaders. Fifty-four men pray and fast one day a month on behalf of their pastor. A team of prayer warriors also prays for the leaders during the worship services. Unquestionably, this church is a praying church.

The church hasn't always had this commitment to pray for their staff, though. Listen to Pastor Guernsey's words:

> As clergy we need people to pray for us. But there has been reluctance on the part of clergy to seek the prayer we need, and second, there is ignorance on the part of the laity as to the importance of covering the clergy in prayer. . . . The first step in getting the prayer support I needed was repentance. I needed to repent from the pulpit for my failure to seek the prayer I needed and for failing to be open and forthright. Then I needed to preach and teach consistently about praying for me and explicitly to ask for the prayers from my people.[1]

---

[1]Cited in *Connected: The Bimonthly Newsletter of the National Association of Local Church Prayer Leaders* (June 2002): 3.

All Saints Episcopal is now a church led by a pastor who intentionally seeks the prayer support of his members. Together they have become a prayer-driven congregation.

WHY LEADERS NEED PRAYER SUPPORT

I have served as a pastor for almost twenty years. If I could make one change in my ministry over those years, it would be to do what Pastor Guernsey did—ask and expect my members to pray for me in a more intentional way. I always knew there were a few prayer warriors interceding for me (you'll hear about some of them later), but I wonder how my ministry would have been different if others had been specifically praying as well.

I now have the privilege of teaching at a seminary. You may think seminary professors don't need much prayer, but I've found that I have the same needs here as I do in the local church. For several reasons, all who lead the church in any capacity need prayer:

God Holds Leaders to High Standards

The Bible speaks clearly about expectations for those who lead the church. Those who minister should be full of the Spirit and wisdom (Acts 6:3). Leaders are to train themselves in godliness (1 Timothy 4:7). Pastors are expected to be above reproach (1 Timothy 3:2). Moreover, James 3:1 warns us that teachers will be judged more strictly than others.

Who among us can live up to these expectations? The answer, of course, is that none of us can. We can't be the people God wants us to be, nor can we do what he wants us to do, apart from prayer. No wonder Paul so often asked believers to pray for him (see Ephesians 6:18–19; Colossians 4:3; 1 Thessalonians 5:25; 2 Thessalonians 3:1–2).

Leaders Are Sometimes Guilty of the "Do Good, but with No Power" Syndrome

Let's be honest. Most of us who are leaders in churches are gifted enough to carry out our responsibilities *in our own strength*—at least for a while. We know how to "do good." What's more, we usually have enough years in church work that our experience covers up many of our shortcomings. Our own prayer life becomes less important because we become less dependent on the power of God.

Here's how E. M. Bounds described this problem among preachers, though his words certainly apply to any church leader:

> Preachers of the present age excel those of the past in many, possibly in all, human elements of success. They are well abreast of the age in learning, research, and intellectual vigor. But these things neither ensure power from on high nor guarantee a righteous life or a thriving religious experience. . . . The presence of these earthly talents, even in the most commanding and impressive form and richest measure, do not in the least abate the necessity for the added endowment of the Holy Spirit. . . . All around us we see a tendency to substitute human gifts and worldly attainments for that supernatural, inward power that comes from heaven in answer to earnest prayer.[2]

---

[2]E. M. Bounds, *The Weapon of Prayer* (Springdale, Pa.: Whitaker House, 1996), 128–29.

Is it possible that you are guilty of the "do good, but with no power" syndrome? Ask a group of intercessors to pray this prayer for you: "Lord, help _____ never to lead our church in his or her own strength. Give all of us grace to recognize our need for *your* power." Church leaders who pray this way are moving their church toward being a praying church.

The Enemy Aims His Darts at Leaders

Satan knows that fallen leaders result in discouraged, disappointed followers. Sadly, though, we often don't pray much for church leaders until *after* we hear that they've been caught in an immoral situation. The word gets out, and then we start praying. By that point, the Enemy has most often already won.

One pastor of a church in Ohio discovered through a church health survey that only 27 percent of his congregation's members were praying daily for him and his family.[3] He assumed the survey would show as many as 75 to 80 percent of the people engaged in prayer, so he was shocked to find out how few people pray for him each day. Knowing that the Enemy shoots at unprotected believers and their families, he quickly developed strategies to get his church praying for him. Some of those strategies can be found in the next section of this chapter.

PRAYING FOR OUR CHURCH LEADERS

Several years ago, Peter Wagner wrote a book about intercessory prayer called *Prayer Shield: How to Intercede for Pastors, Christian*

---

[3]For information about the church health survey we recommend, see the Website for Church Central, Inc. (www.churchcentral.com) or for the Rainer Group (www.rainergroup.com).

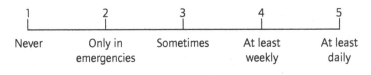

Leaders and Others on the Spiritual Frontlines.[4] What do you think of when you hear words like *shield* and *front lines*? Most likely you think of a battle—and that's Wagner's point. Church leaders who are under attack by the Enemy need prayer support in order to stand firm in the battle. Following are several ways to pray for your church's leaders:

Leader's Prayer Partners

One of the most effective methods for praying for leaders is to enlist a group of "Leader's Prayer Partners." Popularized first as "Pastor's Prayer Partners," the approach has been broadened to include other leaders in the church. These prayer partners agree to pray daily for a church leader for a renewable, specified period of time (three months, for example).

If you're interested in helping your church develop a "Leader's Prayer Partners" ministry, there are five steps you may want to follow. First, *start with the well-known prayer warriors in your church.* You may discover that members are already praying consistently for leaders, but no one has organized or focused these efforts.

---

[4]C. Peter Wagner, *Prayer Shield: How to Intercede for Pastors, Christian Leaders and Others on the Spiritual Frontlines* (Ventura, Calif.: Regal, 1992).

Second, *recruit other pray-ers.* Find the best way to enlist others to join the prayer team. For example, leaders of the Manna Church in Fayetteville, North Carolina, sponsored a "Prayer Shield Sunday" and encouraged members to sign up to pray for all eight of their pastors. Each participant also received a bookmark reminder that included prayer requests.[5]

Jan Niel, prayer leader at Frazer Memorial United Methodist Church in Montgomery, Alabama, asks prospective prayer partners to come to a dinner with the pastor and invites them to make a commitment to serve.[6] In other cases, the church leaders themselves handpick prayer partners who can be trusted to deal sensitively with personal prayer requests.

As you recruit other pray-ers, remember that leaders other than the pastor also need prayer support. Other staff members, deacons, elders, Bible study teachers, church school teachers, small group leaders—all these and others will appreciate intercessory prayer for their ministries. A prayer-driven church finds a way to pray strategically for as many leaders as possible.

Third, *secure a commitment from the partners and train them.* The "Prayer Partner Commitment Card" is a simple way to record each partner's commitment to the ministry. Don't assume, though, that each partner is fully prepared to pray effectively. Train the partners, perhaps using some of the resources noted in this book. Work hard to build a team among the prayer warriors.

Fourth, *keep prayer partners informed.* Prayer warriors who know that their prayers are making a difference will stay in the

---

[5]Cited in *Connected: The Bimonthly Newsletter of the National Association of Local Church Prayer Leaders* (December 2001): 4.

[6]Cited in *Empowered: An Equipping Journal for Local Church Prayer Leaders* (Fall 2001): 17.

Prayer Partner Commitment Card

I, _____, commit to pray for

_____ , who is serving as a church

leader in the role of _____ .

From now until _____, I will

- pray daily for _____ and his or her ministry.
- pray as soon as possible for _____ when emergency needs arise.
- attend training events as scheduled, unless providentially hindered.
- encourage others to pray for _____ and the ministry.
- inform the prayer partner leader if I cannot fulfill these commitments.

_____   _____
Signed   Date

battle longer. Consistently (daily, weekly) inform them about prayer needs. Most important of all, let them know about answered prayers. Write e-mail messages to give immediate information. Plan monthly or quarterly get-togethers to encourage the partners to maintain the prayer shield around the church's leaders.

Fifth, *show appreciation for the prayer partners.* Terry Teykl, executive director of Renewal Ministries and author of several books on prayer, encourages churches to recognize prayer partners at least once or twice a year.[7] Recognize them from the

---

[7]Terry Teykl, *Preyed On or Prayed For* (Muncie, Ind.: PrayerPoint, 2000), 116.

pulpit. Encourage leaders to send personal thank-you notes. Hold a banquet to honor the partners. Plan a service where the partners are the recipients of the church's prayers. Any public recognition will affirm the present prayer partners and encourage others to become part of the church's prayer shield.

Other Prayer Strategies for Church Leaders

"Leader's Prayer Partners" is an effective way to organize prayer for your church's leaders, but your congregation may not yet be ready to tackle this type of ministry. If not, be willing to start small. Consider other ways to pray for your leaders:

❏ Develop prayer partners for only one staff member—the pastor—and then add other leaders when it seems feasible.

❏ Publicize the leaders' birthdays and anniversaries. Pray specifically for them on these significant days.

❏ Call an annual one-day prayer and fasting emphasis to intercede for the church staff and other appropriate leaders.

❏ Take one week per month to pray specifically for particular leaders of the church. For example, pray one week for the deacons when the church is preparing to choose additional deacons. Take one week to pray for Bible study teachers when they begin a new year of service.

❏ Encourage each adult and youth church school class or small group to pray for a different leader each week.

❏ If your church has a Website, establish a prayer site for leaders to share their prayer requests. Teach members to access the requests and pray for the needs.

❏ Publish an annual list of leaders, and ask members to pray through the list as the Lord leads them.
❏ When new leaders are enlisted, hold a prayer and commissioning service especially for them.

Activity #2: Review the list of ways to promote prayer for leaders. Which do you think might work well in your church?

PRAYING FOR OTHER LEADERS

This chapter has focused on church leaders, but the Bible also calls us to pray for "kings and all those in authority, that we may live peaceful and quiet lives in all godliness and holiness" (1 Timothy 2:2). Regrettably, many church members pray for political authorities only during times of election or crisis, though the Bible doesn't limit our prayer mandate to those times.

Prayer-driven churches intercede not only for church leaders but also for government officials. In many cases, one of the stations in the church's prayer room can cover this area (see chapter 3). The World Prayer Center at New Life Church in Colorado Springs, Colorado, includes a separate station called "Authorities." At Ash Street Baptist Church in Forest Park, Georgia, church and political leaders are included in the same station. The prayer room at Johnson's Ferry Baptist Church in Marietta, Georgia, contains a notebook with names of national, state, county, city, and local officials, including the principals of the local schools.

Thousands of churches also pray for government leaders on the National Day of Prayer, held on the first Thursday of May each year. In fact, citywide interdenominational prayer events were held in more than sixty cities during the 2002 National Day of Prayer.[8] Observing the local NDP in your area is one way to involve your church in praying for community and political leaders. See the resources included in the back of this book, which will help you with this task as well.

Praying for Political Leaders[9]

1. Pray for just leaders who will rule in the fear of God.
2. Pray for leaders who will be free from covetousness and immorality and will not misuse power, position, or possessions.
3. Pray for leaders who will be wise and have a teachable spirit.
4. Pray for leaders who will lead with mercy and truth.
5. Pray for leaders who will be free from bribery, corruption, and flattery.
6. Pray for leaders who will be charitable and compassionate and have a heart for the poor.
7. Pray for others who will have opportunity to influence leaders for good.

CONCLUSION

Two prayer warriors who have left a mark on my life are Ruby Floyd and Bobbie Byrd. Both women prayed diligently for me when I served as their pastor in two different churches, and I'm convinced my ministry was stronger because of the prayers of

[8]National Day of Prayer Website (www.nationaldayofprayer.org). Another resource is the Website for Intercessors for America (www.ifa-usapray.org).

[9]Adapted from Elaine Helms, *If My People . . . Pray* (Marietta, Ga.: Church Prayer Ministries, 2000), 59.

these women. Whether they were praying for me, for other church leaders, or for our nation's leaders, I knew I wanted these prayer warriors on our side.

Today I always ask God to give me someone like Ruby or Bobbie when he calls me to a new ministry. I'm also praying that God allows all of my students to have such a prayer warrior in their churches.

How many other leaders, I wonder, *long to have these kinds of people support them in prayer?* I suspect there are thousands of church leaders who need the support of at least one prayer partner who will touch heaven on their behalf.

Are you willing to be that kind of prayer warrior? If you are, your church will be one step closer to being a prayer-driven church.

QUESTIONS FOR REFLECTION AND DISCUSSION

1. Read Hebrews 13:17. Why is it important that we pray for those who lead us in the church?

2. If your church doesn't have a "Leader's Prayer Partners" ministry in place, what obstacles do you see to beginning one? How might you help overcome them? If you do have a ministry, how might it be strengthened?

3. What specific strategy does your church have to pray for political leaders? If there is none, what might you do to help the church address this need?

4. As a group, covenant together to pray for your leaders as you continue this study. Note specific concerns for which you could pray.

FIVE

Praying Evangelistically

Who was praying for you to become a Christian when you first realized your need to follow God? A parent? A grandparent? A friend? Your pastor? An entire church?

My classmate Randy first told me about Jesus when I was twelve years old. Every day during my seventh-grade year, he told me about my need to follow Jesus Christ. In fact, I thought he was a little radical with his religion; he knew I was going to hell—and he wasn't afraid to tell me so!

I successfully ignored Randy and his message until the end of the school year. The summer, I thought, would bring a needed break from his "religious stuff." What I didn't realize was that Randy was praying for me throughout the summer. At the same time, my Christian neighbors had begun to pray for my family. Unbeknownst to me as well, my grandma was also praying for my salvation.

What do you suppose happened to me toward the end of the summer? Jesus saved me and made me his child, and my life has never been the same. The fervent prayers of God's people made a difference.

WHY PRAYER MATTERS IN EVANGELISM

Pastor Gary Kinnaman leads a 5:30 A.M. weekly men's prayer meeting at the Word of Grace Church in Mesa, Arizona. The group has two rules: members must commit for six months, and they must be present each week unless they're ill or out of town. Attendance is taken, and group members hold each other accountable when they miss.[1] Pastor Kinnaman knows that prayer really does matter, and he's training his church to make prayer a priority.

Why does prayer matter so much, particularly with regard to evangelism? To put it simply, we'll never reach people for Jesus Christ apart from the power of God.

The Bible is clear about the state of nonbelievers. They are held in the "dominion of darkness" (Colossians 1:13), "condemned already" (John 3:18), and blinded by "the god of this age" (2 Corinthians 4:4). They usually hold on to lies, such as "there is no God" or "I'm good enough for God to accept me." No human power or intellect is strong enough to move them from darkness to light or from deception to truth. Only prayer can work these miracles.

HOW TO PRAY EVANGELISTICALLY

Most effective evangelistic churches pray *intentionally*—that is, they have a prayer strategy with focus and direction. They pray both for believers who are engaged in evangelism and for nonbelievers they are trying to reach.

Pray for Believers to Be Witnesses

If anybody knew about the need for prayer support, it was the apostle Paul. God called him to tell the good news about Jesus, and his obedience landed him in jail. Yet, Paul never ran

---

[1] Cited in Gary Kinnaman, "A Reason to Pray," *Pray!* 30 (May/June 2002): 17. This magazine is an important resource for prayer leaders. See www.praymag.com.

from the battle. Instead, he asked the believers in the regions of Ephesus and Colosse to pray for him:

> Pray also for me, that whenever I open my mouth, words may be given me so that I will fearlessly make known the mystery of the gospel, for which I am an ambassador in chains. Pray that I may declare it fearlessly, as I should.
>
> —Ephesians 6:19 – 20

> Devote yourselves to prayer, being watchful and thankful. And pray for us, too, that God may open a door for our message, so that we may proclaim the mystery of Christ, for which I am in chains. Pray that I may proclaim it clearly, as I should.
>
> —Colossians 4:2 – 4

Paul is a spiritual hero to many of us. He preached the gospel to kings, and he willingly suffered for his faith. Yet even he needed prayer support to proclaim the gospel boldly and clearly. If Paul needed that kind of prayer, is it possible that we might need prayer support, too?

I recently heard about a Christian inmate in Brazil who was badly beaten and threatened with death. Believers around the world began to pray for him. God healed him and allowed him to return to the general prison population, where he continued

---

Activity #1: Read Ephesians 6:19 – 20 and Colossians 4:2 – 4 again. List Paul's specific requests for prayer. Spend a few moments thinking about these requests. Do you have anyone praying this way for you?

to witness and teach Bible studies. In response to the prayers of his people, God gave the inmate boldness, even in the face of death. In fact, his courage and steadfastness so influenced a satanist in the prison that the satanist recently became a believer![2]

If your church wants to pray evangelistically, begin by enlisting prayer partners to pray Ephesians 6:19–20 and Colossians 4:2–4 for each other. Provide magnetic prayer reminder cards like this one:

Prayer Reminder Card

I commit myself to pray daily for _____
so that he or she may share Jesus Christ boldly and clearly when God gives opportunities.

> Pray also for me, that whenever I open my mouth, words may
> be given me so that I will fearlessly make known the mystery of
> the gospel.... Pray that I may declare it fearlessly, as I should.
>
> —Ephesians 6:19–20

> Devote yourselves to prayer, being watchful and thankful.
> And pray for us, too, that God may open a door for our message,
> so that we may proclaim the mystery of Christ.... Pray that I may
> proclaim it clearly, as I should.
>
> —Colossians 4:2–4

Pray for God to Change the Hearts of Nonbelievers

Prayer-driven churches understand that only God produces the harvest of evangelism (1 Corinthians 3:6–7), so they must

---

[2]Cited in "A Window on the World: Living proof," *The Commission*, 65 no. 4 (June 2002): 4.

Listen to the pastors of growing churches describe their church's experience with prayer for the lost:

"We have a prayer room where members volunteer one hour per week to pray specifically for lost people." —Florida

"We keep a prayer list for salvation. After a person is converted, the name stays on the list as the church continues to pray for real spiritual growth." —Idaho

"Every week one person from each Sunday school class is selected to go to the prayer room and pray specifically for the lost to be converted." —Florida

"Our growth through conversions? It's the result of our prayer ministry that takes place seven days a week." —Kentucky

pray. For example, members of the First Southern Baptist Church of Lompoc, California, are encouraged each week to submit the name of a lost person.[3] The church staff prays each Sunday evening for the names submitted, and other groups pray on Saturday evenings for nonbelievers. The church is an evangelistic church, but they know that their efforts are fruitless apart from God. They realize that only God can change a heart.

Our research at the Billy Graham School shows that evangelistic churches pray for lost persons by name, echoing the prayer of Paul in Romans 10:1 — "My heart's desire and prayer to God for the Israelites is that they may be saved." One church we studied has *four thousand* names on their prayer list, even though they average only two hundred in worship attendance—*and*

---

[3]Stories and quotes in this section are found in Thom S. Rainer, *Effective Evangelistic Churches* (Nashville: Broadman & Holman, 1995), 66–69.

even though they require members to witness first to the people whose names are placed on the list! How does your church compare to this church?

Activity #2: On a scale of 1 to 10 (1 = very weak and 10 = very strong), rate your church's commitment to praying intentionally for nonbelievers.

```
1     2     3     4     5     6     7     8     9     10
├─────┼─────┼─────┼─────┼─────┼─────┼─────┼─────┼─────┤
```

STRATEGIES FOR PRAYING EVANGELISTICALLY

Chapter 7 includes many ideas for incorporating prayer into your church. For now, though, let's look at three strategies that relate specifically to evangelism:

Prayerwalking

Prayerwalking is exactly what it sounds like—believers walking and praying. *Incidental prayerwalking* occurs when God prompts us to pray for others as we're working throughout the day. *Intentional prayerwalking* includes planned and organized times for on-site praying.[4] The intentional method may be as simple as praying for people as you walk through their neighborhoods or as complicated as leading a prayer team overseas. Prayerwalking allows us to see more clearly with God's eyes the people he has called us to reach.

---

[4]As defined in the "Prayerwalking" brochure, International Mission Board, Southern Baptist Convention.

The Armitage Baptist Church of Chicago, Illinois, is one example of a church that intentionally prayerwalks their neighborhood. Each year, 150 to 200 members walk the streets of Chicago, praying as a large group, as "squadrons" of 30 to 45 people, or as "triplets." They've prayed in places where gangs have been in control, where drug dealers have operated, and where young teens have been killed. Though the prayerwalks aren't intentionally evangelistic, they often open the door to further outreach in those communities.[5]

Your church may not be located in an inner-city neighborhood, but any congregation can adapt the following prayerwalking steps to fit their context:

- ❏ Determine the area to walk (perhaps a subdivision, an apartment complex, a downtown neighborhood, or a shopping mall).
- ❏ Be sensitive to God's Spirit—keep your eyes and ears open to see and to hear needs in the community. For example, pray for the students and faculty when you pass a school. Pray for the patients and staff when you pass a hospital. Pray for the departing and incoming families when you see a "For Sale" sign in a front yard.
- ❏ Be prepared to share your faith if an opportunity arises during the walk.
- ❏ If possible, meet with other walkers to give a report after the prayerwalk. Talk specifically about what you learned about the community. Begin to develop a plan to follow up with outreach and evangelism.

---

[5]Cited in Charles Lyons, "The Prayer Hood," *Leadership* (Fall 2001): 66–68.

❏ Lay out a strategy to prayerwalk targeted areas of your community each year. Set a goal to cover the entire community with prayer within a reasonable amount of time.

Lighthouses of Prayer

Patrick is a member of an Evangelical Free church. Dismayed by their own lack of evangelism vision, he and his wife attended a conference on the "Lighthouses of Prayer" movement. While there they heard these words over and over again: *"Prayer, care, and share* if you want to reach your neighbors."

Patrick and his wife began to pray daily for five of their neighbors, and they looked for opportunities to minister to them through good deeds. Sometimes they offered to baby-sit their neighbors' children. Patrick mowed his neighbors' yards. His wife made desserts for the neighborhood. At the end of six months, two of the neighbors had become Christians as a result of Patrick and his wife being a "lighthouse" in the community.

A *lighthouse of prayer* is "a gathering of two or more people in Jesus' name for the purpose of praying for, caring for, and sharing Christ with their neighbors and others in their sphere of influence."[6] Essentially, believers *pray* for their neighbors by name, *care* for them through ministry, and *share* Jesus with them. Focused, consistent prayer among believers is the foundation for everything else that takes place.

The Union Chapel United Methodist congregation in Muncie, Indiana, is a praying church. They have over 150 members who serve as the "prayer army" interceding for their staff. In addition, over one hundred families serve as lighthouses of

---

[6]Paul A. Cedar, "The Lighthouse Movement," *Pray!* 15 (Nov/Dec 1999):18. See also www.lighthousemovement.com.

prayer in their community. Listen to this evaluation of the light-house approach from associate pastor Glenn Greiner: "Light-houses of prayer is the most effective, easiest to manage, and doable prayer/evangelism strategy I've seen."[7]

Perhaps your church might consider this strategy. Begin by praying for your own neighbors, asking God to

❏ minister to their spiritual, emotional, and physical needs.
❏ give you opportunities to get to know them.
❏ show you ways to meet their needs.
❏ make you bold enough to witness to them.
❏ open the blinded minds of nonbelievers in your neighborhood.

Activity #3: List the names of three to five neighbors for whom you and your family will be a "lighthouse." Pray that others in your church will consider using this important outreach strategy.

Targeted Praying

Pastor Bob Beckett of the Dwelling Place Church in Hemet, California, directs his church to pray "smart bomb" prayers rather than "scud missile" prayers. If you remember the Persian Gulf War, you'll understand Beckett's terminology. The Iraqi scud missiles were often misguided and inaccurate, but the "smart bombs" of the allied forces hit their targets with incredible precision. Maybe you remember seeing videoclips of smart bombs that were guided directly into the enemy's buildings.

"Smart bomb" praying is precise, with a clear target and a recognized goal. Beckett uses the terminology to mean prayer

---

[7]Personal correspondence with Brett Champion, research assistant.

primarily aimed against demonic forces, but the concept can generally be applied to all praying. We pray most effectively when our prayers are intentional and focused.

Think about all the groups in your community for whom you might intentionally focus your prayers. Teachers. Politicians. Police officers. Firefighters. Mail carriers. Bankers. Hairdressers. Teenagers. City employees. Store clerks. Bus drivers. What might happen if churches in a community committed to interceding for a different group each quarter of the calendar year? Not only will we pray with more focused passion, but our burden for reaching out to these groups will also likely increase.

One of the missionaries on my prayer list is Randy, who is serving in Moscow, Russia. His primary responsibility is to reach out to the policemen and the military officers stationed in that massive city. I suppose I could pray for God to reach all of the people in Moscow, but my prayers have been much more passionate when centered on the particular sphere of Randy's ministry.

Prayer-driven churches focus their evangelistic prayers like a laser beam. Does your church pray for lost people with this kind of focus and fire?

CONCLUSION

If your church doesn't pray intentionally about evangelism, now is the time to begin. Use the following acronym as a guide to pray for believers and nonbelievers. Pray that your church will have **GOD'S HEART**.[8]

---

[8]The "HEART" portion of this acronym is taken from Chris Schofield, *Praying Your Friends to Christ* (Alpharetta, Ga.: North American Mission Board, 1997).

G = Pray that believers will appreciate **God's grace**. Only when we really appreciate what God has done for us will we be best prepared to tell others about him.

O = Pray that believers will be **obedient**. Disobedience hinders our prayers (Isaiah 59:1–2), while obedience demands that we engage in evangelism.

D' = Pray that believers will have a **desire** to tell others. How can we keep to ourselves the good news about Jesus?

S = Pray that believers will **speak** the gospel fearlessly and clearly—remember Paul's prayer requests in Ephesians 6 and Colossians 4?

H = Pray for nonbelievers to have a receptive **heart** to the gospel. Only God can make this happen.

E = Pray that their spiritual **eyes** will be opened. Remember, they are blinded to the truth (2 Corinthians 4:3–4).

A = Pray that they will have God's **attitude** toward sin. Genuine repentance is possible only when lost people see their sin as God sees it.

R = Pray that they will be **released** to believe. God alone reaps the harvest by freeing nonbelievers from the domain of darkness (Colossians 1:13).

T = Pray that their lives will be **transformed**. Salvation results in a changed life.

QUESTIONS FOR REFLECTION AND DISCUSSION

1. What steps do you and your church need to take to pray more passionately about evangelism?

2. Read Luke 19:41 –44 to see Jesus' grief over the unbelieving city of Jerusalem. Is your heart broken over the nonbelievers in your city? If not, ask God to give you the heart of Jesus.

3. Choose one of the suggested prayer strategies in this chapter. What steps might you take to begin implementing this strategy in your church?

4. Who were the people who were praying for you when you weren't a believer? Thank God for them, and then continue their pattern by praying for others.

SIX

Multiplying Pray-ers in Your Church

Several months ago I talked to a student who was less than a year away from beginning full-time ministry. "You know, Doc," he said, "I'm not sure I know how to pray. I'm really trying to do what I'm supposed to do, but nobody's ever taught me how to pray. So I don't know if I'm doing what I should or not."

This young man had been raised in church, had attended small group discipleship studies for men, and had now been in seminary for two years. Yet, he still wasn't sure he knew how to pray, because no one had taken the time to teach him how to pray.

Compare my student's story to the way Jesus trained his disciples. When Jesus called his followers, he *expected* much from them; he told them to deny themselves and follow him (Mark 8:34; Matthew 4:18–20). He *taught* them, and his teachings were often penetrating and life-changing (Matthew 5–7). He built a *relationship* with them while also calling them to love one another (John 15:9–12). And he *involved* them in ministry by challenging them and sending them out (Luke 9:12–17; 10:1–16).

We might picture Jesus' training methods as the four corners of a training rectangle:

73

Of course, we know it's always best to follow Jesus' methods. As your church trains and multiplies prayer warriors, be sure to incorporate each of these four components into your strategy. "Our Strategy for Multiplying Pray-ers" (appendix 5) will help you with this process.

EXPECT YOUR CHURCH MEMBERS TO PRAY

Does the Bible expect believers to pray? Look at these clues and decide for yourself:

- ❑ Matthew 6:6—"When you pray, go into your room . . ."
- ❑ Luke 18:1—"Jesus told his disciples a parable to show them that they should always pray and not give up."
- ❑ Philippians 4:6—"In everything, by prayer and petition, with thanksgiving, present your requests to God."
- ❑ 1 Thessalonians 5:17—"Pray continually."
- ❑ James 5:16—"Pray for each other so that you may be healed. The prayer of a righteous man is powerful and effective."

From these Scriptures and others, we see that God simply *expects* his church to be a house of prayer (Isaiah 56:7). There are several effective ways to get this message across to your church.

First, *make sure that your church's covenant or mission statement emphasizes prayer.* Many church covenants only assume that church members will be praying members. Others, like the example at the top of page 75, include prayer as a specific expectation for their members.

Second, *incorporate prayer training into your church's new-member training.* One of our studies at the Billy Graham School

1. I will strengthen the testimony of the church by

   - studying and following God's Word.
   - praying consistently for church leaders, other members, and nonbelievers.
   - living my life in a God-honoring way.

2. I will seek and take advantage of opportunities to tell others of the good news about Jesus—including supporting and praying for missionaries around the world.

showed that only 35 percent of growing churches include an introduction to the spiritual disciplines in their new-member class.[1] Yet what better opportunity is there to teach new members and young believers how to pray?

Pastor Jessie Charpentier of Pine First Baptist Church in Franklinton, Louisiana, includes prayer as one of nine major topics in his church's new-believer class. He teaches new believers how to have a "holy hour" with God. Listen to this pastor's passionate expectation of new members: "Prayer is hard work! Don't be afraid to put some effort and energy into your personal time alone with God."[2] I suspect that new believers in this church will pray more just because they're learning that prayer is *expected* of them.

A third way to raise expectations for prayer is to *give more significance to the church prayer meeting.* Greg Frizzell, author of eight books about prayer and spiritual awakening, rightly argues that the prayer meeting is no longer a priority in most

[1]Thom S. Rainer, *Surprising Insights from the Unchurched* (Grand Rapids: Zondervan, 2001), 113–14.

[2]Cited in *The New Believer's Class Notebook*, Pine First Baptist Church, Franklinton, Louisiana.

churches. He contends that the loss of corporate prayer has had a profound negative impact on the power of today's church, and thus he calls the church back to prayer.[3]

In the late nineteenth century, Charles Spurgeon also challenged pastors to focus on corporate prayer.[4] Using the chart on the following page, compare Spurgeon's and Frizzell's ideas for improving a prayer meeting. Mark the ideas that can strengthen your church's prayer meetings.

Remember the stories of corporate prayer in the Metropolitan Tabernacle and Brooklyn Tabernacle in chapter 1. People who came to these churches knew they would be praying there. Praying churches make corporate prayer a priority and expect their members to pray.

Activity #1: On a scale of 1 to 10 (1 = poor and 10 = excellent), rate the overall effectiveness of your church's prayer meetings.

| 1 | 2 | 3 | 4 | 5 | 6 | 7 | 8 | 9 | 10 |

TEACH YOUR MEMBERS TO PRAY

The second corner of our strategy for multiplying pray-ers — *teaching* — reflects an elementary educational principle: People usually don't learn what we don't teach them. One way to make sure that our churches *aren't* prayer-driven is to fail to teach about prayer.

---

[3]See Greg Frizzell, *Biblical Patterns for Powerful Church Prayer Meetings* (Memphis: Master Design, 1999), 12. In the chart, Frizzell's ideas for prayer meetings are taken from *Biblical Patterns*.

[4]Charles H. Spurgeon, *Only a Prayer Meeting* (Great Britain: Christian Focus Publications, 2000), 17–21.

How to Improve Prayer Meetings

Spurgeon

1. The minister must himself put a high value on the prayer meeting.

2. Don't let individual members dominate the prayer time.

3. Persuade everybody to pray aloud—it will be good for all.

4. Encourage the attenders to submit special requests for prayer; these scraps of paper "may be used as kindling to the fire in the whole assembly."

5. Don't let anything else (hymns, chapters, addresses) supplant prayer.

6. Two or three brethren may succeed each other in prayer without pause, but do so judiciously.

7. Lead the congregation to identify and pray for the key kingdom issues.

8. Schedule additional prayer meetings for your more fervent intercessors.

9. Promote the weekly meeting as a time of joy and life-changing power.

Frizzell

1. Give prayerful planning to the weekly prayer meeting.

2. Promote the weekly prayer meeting as genuine top priority.

3. View the prayer meeting as a "relationship encounter" with God.

4. Use the weekly prayer meeting to grow your people in intercession. *Teach* believers how to intercede.

5. Schedule significant prayer time in the weekly meeting.

6. Focus prayer mostly on issues that are eternal rather than temporal.

Teaching about prayer can take place at several levels. Your pastor may choose to preach an annual sermon series, such as "Prayer Warriors in the Bible," "Great Prayers of the Bible," or "Jesus on Prayer." Your small groups might do a quarterly study on prayer. Your church might also sponsor community-wide prayer conferences that bring together prayer warriors from around your city.

A "College of Prayer" is another option. "College of Prayer" churches offer several courses on prayer (typically, six to twelve weeks for each), and members who successfully complete all the courses receive a certificate or diploma. Use some of the resources listed in this book as the curriculum, or consider producing your own courses:

❏ Course 101: What the Bible Says about Prayer
❏ Course 102: Methods and Models of Prayer
❏ Course 103: Why the Lord Doesn't Answer Our Prayers
❏ Course 104: Spiritual Warfare Prayer

If your church doesn't have the resources to establish a "College of Prayer," you probably still have the most important resource for teaching about prayer, namely, people who pray. Find one or two people who are committed to prayer, and challenge them to teach two others in the church. The teaching might be informal or formal, but the goal is still to multiply the pray-ers.

My friend Shirley Smith is a prayer warrior extraordinaire in Texas. She's one of those persons you call when you need to know for sure that God is listening. Many years ago, Shirley taught me about praying out loud while driving. The concept

Activity #2: In your opinion, how much does your church teach about prayer, either in worship services or in small group Bible studies?

_____ A lot—at least once a month

_____ Occasionally—once or twice every three months

_____ Not much—once or twice a year

_____ Never

was simple, but I just hadn't thought about using my time in the car so wisely. "I just talk to God as though he's in the passenger seat," Shirley said.

Many years later, I still use this method that Shirley taught me, and I tell this story when I lead prayer conferences. Shirley Smith (one person) taught me (one person), and now I have the privilege of teaching others. Start with one or two teachers, and then trust God to multiply the pray-ers in your church.

TEACH AND MODEL PRAYER IN THE CONTEXT OF <u>RELATIONSHIPS</u>

The third corner of the multiplication strategy is *relationships.* To understand the importance of relationships, think back to the passages in Luke's gospel you studied in chapter 1. Luke 3:21– 22 tells us that Jesus was praying when the Holy Spirit descended on him like a dove at his baptism. Luke 5:16 indicates that Jesus often withdrew from the crowds in order to pray. Jesus prayed all night before calling his disciples, according to Luke 6:12. It was during a prayer time that Jesus was changed miraculously in front of Peter, James, and John (Luke 9:28–29).

Can you imagine hearing Jesus pray, and then seeing God doing mighty things in response? No wonder the disciples said to him, "Lord, teach us to pray" (Luke 11:1)!

Here's the point—Jesus taught his disciples how to pray *in the context of a relationship.* He didn't just lecture to them as a professor who teaches one day and then doesn't see the students again until the next class. Though Jesus had private times of prayer, his disciples were often with him when he prayed (Luke 9:28–29). Sometimes he simply told them he was going away to pray (Mark 14:32). They heard him pray with joy at times (Luke 10:21), but they also knew his deep sorrow in prayer at other times (Mark 14:32–34).

Jesus didn't just teach them prayer. He also *lived prayer* in front of them. That, I believe, is what we must do if we want to multiply pray-ers in our churches. We have to teach and model prayer in the context of relationships.

Of course, the most important relationship context for teaching prayer is the family, and the most significant teachers of prayer should be parents. Here are a few ways to become a prayer-driven family:

❏ Make prayer a habit in your home. Set a time and a place, and make prayer a priority.

❏ Give your children a prayer calendar. Help them think about important events in their lives (school tests, field trips, friends' birthdays, and so forth) and then pray about the events.

❏ Set the example. Let your children see and hear you pray (especially you fathers!).

❏ Allow children to make a prayer poster for each week. List prayer needs, and hang the poster in the child's bedroom.

❏ Encourage your pastor and church leaders to offer training on leading family devotions.

Another effective way to build prayer within relationships is to develop a mentoring program for new believers. Mentoring, which I define as "a God-given relationship in which one growing Christian encourages and equips another believer to reach his or her potential as a disciple of Christ,"[5] provides a context for teaching *and* modeling prayer. New believers learn much as they watch mature Christians relate to God in prayer.

In a variation on praying in relationships, the Berean Fellowship in Toledo, Ohio, has a "Secret Prayer Pal Ministry" for adult ladies and girls ages six to eighteen. From September to May, each girl has a secret adult "prayer pal" with whom she shares prayer concerns, exchanges small gifts, and writes letters. In May, the secret prayer pals are revealed, and girls and women alike have developed new friendships—and they've probably gained long-term prayer support as well.[6]

INTENTIONALLY GET MEMBERS <u>INVOLVED</u> IN THE PRAYER MINISTRY

The final corner of our strategy for multiplying pray-ers is *involvement.* What might seem obvious—namely, that people have to be involved somewhere in the prayer ministry in order to grow—isn't always so easily accomplished. Many church

---

[5]Chuck Lawless, *Making Disciples through Mentoring* (Lynchburg, Va.: Church Growth Institute, 2002), introduction.

[6]Cited in Michele Howe, "Prayer Pal Ministry," *Pray* 3 (November/December, 1997): 13.

members will verbally support a prayer ministry while still doing very little in the ministry itself.

In fact, most people probably won't get involved in a prayer ministry until you work to get them personally involved. Pulpit announcements and bulletin inserts are a start, but nothing works quite as well as personal recruiting.

Prayer-driven churches have leaders who recruit like Jesus did—they expect people to get involved. Set a goal for the percentage of active members you want involved in the prayer ministry over the next year. Establish an annual prayer event/training calendar, and personally invite members to participate in particular events. Enlist others to do follow-up and to secure commitments from potential participants. Use your best leaders to train and encourage the prayer warriors. Then challenge the prayer warriors to commit to mentoring another member so that multiplication and involvement continue. Above all, *pray* for members to get involved!

Activity #3: List the names of a few church members you will personally invite to get involved in your church's prayer ministry.

CONCLUSION

Missionaries are some of the most passionate people I've ever met. For the most part, they love their work and rejoice in being used by God to reach the world. Invite a missionary to speak to your church, and you're liable to leave the building wondering, "Is it possible that God wants *me* to do something?"

Missionaries simply believe in what they're doing, and they realize that their work will end unless churches raise up and send out new missionaries. Too much is at stake for them *not* to be passionate about their callings.

That's the same kind of commitment we need in order to raise up prayer warriors. If you want your church to be a prayer-driven church, develop a strategy to equip and multiply your prayer warriors. Too much is at stake not to do so.

QUESTIONS FOR REFLECTION AND DISCUSSION

1. Read 1 Thessalonians 5:17 again. Then read 1 Thessalonians 1:2 and 2 Timothy 1:3. What was one reason why Paul had the right to tell the believers to "pray continually"?

2. What are some ways to improve your church's prayer meetings? If your church doesn't have a specific time set aside for prayer, should you consider starting one? When might be the best time and place to meet? Whose support do you need in order to move ahead?

3. Assume that God has called you to mentor a young believer, focusing on teaching him or her to pray. What obstacles do you think you will face? How will you overcome these obstacles?

4. In which corner of the training strategy (expectations, teaching, relationships, involvement) is your church the strongest? The weakest? What steps would you suggest to improve the weak areas?

SEVEN

Praying without Ceasing

uppose you were a first-century Christian in the Greek city of
Thessalonica. The word is spreading—a letter from the apostle
Paul arrived today. You and several other believers gather at the
meeting place, where one of the brothers reads Paul's letter.
One specific phrase toward the end of the letter grabs your atten-
tion: "Pray continually" (1 Thessalonians 5:17).

"Pray *continually*?" you ask yourself. "Why, sometimes it's
hard even to pray *each day*. How can anybody pray continually?"

I must confess that I've asked this question, especially during periods when prayer seemed difficult. I've learned, though,
that prayer is the product of a faithful walk with God. Prayer is
always more constant for me when my relationship with God
is strong and growing.

I've also come to realize that prayer is more consistent
when I vary my prayer patterns. If I follow the same routine
every day (for example, praying through the same prayer list
every day), prayer sometimes becomes little more than a habit.
Maybe that's not the case for you, but I need some variety in the
way I pray.

This chapter includes many more ways to incorporate
prayer into your church besides those mentioned earlier in the
book. I encourage you to use varied methods, recognizing that
no single method will appeal to all of your members. Use as
many methods as needed to get as many members as possible
involved in your prayer ministry.

PRAYER STRATEGIES

Prayer cards—Send written notes to people for whom your church has been praying. The cost is minimal, and the witness in the community can be effective. Let the community know that your church is a praying church.

You've Been Prayed For ...

Dear _____,

We want you to know that your friends at _____ Church have been praying for you. We are praying for God to meet your every need and to take care of you.

Blessings,

"The prayer of a righteous man is powerful and effective."

—James 5:16

Monthly prayer calendar—Distribute a prayer calendar that gives direction for praying each day. This strategy requires considerable advance preparation, but it is an effective way to challenge the church to pray. The calendar on the following page gives an example of one week.

Prayer chain—A prayer chain allows members to share prayer needs with each other via an established line of communication. By means of either telephone calls or e-mail messages, one member of the prayer chain notifies another member, who then informs another, and so forth. Sample guidelines for a daily prayer chain can be found in appendix 6.

JULY

Sunday	Monday	Tuesday	Wednesday	Thursday	Friday	Saturday
1 Pray for your Sunday school teachers	2 Pray for your boss and coworkers	3 Pray for local government officials	4 Pray for your nation's president	5 Pray for military personnel	6 Pray for your pastor's wife on her birthday	7 Pray for the choir as they prepare for the musical
8	9	10	11	12	13	14
15	16	17	18	19	20	21
22	23	24	25	26	27	28
29	30	31				

"Computerized" praying—Take advantage of technology to incorporate prayer into your church. Enlist a computer guru to develop a prayer Website for the church. Create an e-mail prayer chain. Encourage members to use resources like *Pray-Timer*—a tool that includes Bible studies, prayer calendars, and downloadable files—to strengthen their prayer lives.[1]

Prayer tape ministry—Collect taped messages about prayer to distribute to shut-in members and to church members who are interested in prayer. Enlist a detail-oriented member to coordinate the cataloging and distributing of the tapes.

Prayer testimonies—Once every quarter, enlist someone to share a testimony about the power of prayer. Include both those who have received clear responses to prayer and those who have learned to remain faithful even when answers to their prayers aren't what they wanted or expected. Either testimony will challenge members to keep on praying. Offer to interview persons who aren't comfortable speaking alone in front of a crowd.

Prayer progressive dinner—Plan a progressive dinner, but change the focus of the evening. After eating at each home, spend time praying for that family and for the neighbors they are trying to reach. Church school classes and other small groups can use this strategy effectively as a prayer/outreach tool.

"Focus on the family" praying—Each week, invite church members to pray the entire week for a particular family in the church. Introduce the family during a Sunday worship service, share their prayer concerns (as they allow), and challenge members to pray for the family members by name. Use the church bulletin or newsletter to report answered prayers.

---

[1]Information about *PrayTimer* may be found at www.namb.net.

Spouse prayer covenants—Write a prayer covenant for spouses to sign (see sample below). Plan a special service to pray for and support the couples who commit to the covenant. You can use this covenant card with engaged couples as well.

Spouse Prayer Covenant

We, _____ and _____, recognize that God has brought us together and that our marriage is to be a testimony to his love for us. We hereby commit to

- talk openly together about our prayer concerns and needs.
- pray *for* each other daily during our individual times with God.
- pray *with* each other daily at a set time.
- hold each other accountable to this commitment.
- enlist another couple who will also hold us accountable to this commitment.

Signed: _____   _____

Prayer outreach surveys—Do a simple survey in your community, asking just one question: "Our church is praying for our friends and neighbors. Do you have any prayer requests that we might include when we pray?" (See page 90 for a sample Prayer Survey Card.) Be sure to record the necessary information (name, address, phone number, prayer request) so that you can follow up. Making available prayer request cards on an ongoing basis is a nonthreatening way to keep in touch with members of your community who have requested prayer.

Prayer power points—At a designated time during the week, members of your church—wherever they are at that time—pause and pray for a particular need. For example, on Monday at noon they may pray for the evangelist prior to a

Prayer Survey Card

Hi, I'm _____ from _____ Church,
and we're praying for our neighbors. Would you like us to pray about
anything for you?

Prayer Concerns:

Person's Name: _____

Address: _____

_____

Phone Number: _____

Name of Surveyor: _____

Notes: _____

_____

_____

_____

Follow-Up:

Prayer Request Card Sent: _____ Phone Follow-up: _____

series of evangelistic rallies, for a member having surgery that
week, or for a church committee facing a challenging task.

"Drive-by" praying—Train members to pray for each
church they drive by during the week. Pray that the gospel
would be preached in this church and that God would use this
congregation to reach lost people. Challenge members of other
churches to pray for your church in the same way.

"On-purpose" prayer teams—If your church is "purpose-
driven," enlist a prayer team to pray for each of the purposes of
the church. Go back to my opening illustration for an example
of a church that prays this way (see page 13).

"John the Baptist" prayer teams—Train some "forerunners" who pray for others as they prepare for and carry out evangelistic and outreach visits. Some "John the Baptist" prayer teams also pray during outreach events such as an evangelistic rally.

"Aaron and Hur" prayer teams—Based on Exodus 17:8–16, "Aaron and Hur" prayer teams intercede for the pastor and leaders during worship services. Teams of two or three people pray together to "lift up the arms" of every person who has a leadership role in the service. Use these prompts for praying:

❏ At the beginning of the service, thank God for allowing you to worship.

❏ Pray that guests and members will experience a sense of worship and warmth.

❏ Pray for each worship leader as he or she participates.

❏ Ask God to protect and anoint the pastor speaking God's word.

❏ Ask God to open the hearts and minds of those hearing God's word.

Praying the announcements—Challenge members to pray specifically about the information included in the church bulletin or newsletter. For example, pray for the young people and their chaperones when a bulletin announcement gives information about an upcoming mission trip. Pray for the women who will meet next week for their monthly missions meeting.

Fasting prayer—Encourage your church members to skip one meal a day for a specified period of time (one day, one week, one month, a quarter), and use that mealtime specifically for prayer. You may want to provide a prayer guide to focus the church's prayers during these times.

Leadership prayer retreats—If your church has a leadership team (church council, elder board, and the like), challenge them to spend significant amounts of time praying together. Begin their term of service with an off-site one- or two-day retreat that focuses only on praying. Leave the planning and strategizing for later.

Caroling prayerwalk—A variation of a regular prayerwalk, this approach incorporates Christmas caroling during the holiday season. Pray as the choir walks from home to home, and then share the good news about Jesus through singing.

"See you at the pole"—This national event calls for young people to gather around the flagpole at their schools and pray for their classmates, administrators, teachers, nation, and world. This event usually takes place in September.[2]

Moms in Touch—The goal of Moms in Touch is to raise up intercessors for every school in North America. Mothers pray together for one hour per week, asking God to save their children, give them boldness to stand up for their faith, and keep them safe from violence.[3]

"People Group" praying—Through the international missions groups with whom your church works, select an unreached people group and begin praying for them. Learn as much as you can about the group. Travel to minister among them, if possible. An Internet search for "unreached people groups" will provide other information that can guide your praying.

"Senior Saints" intercession—Utilize your senior adults, including shut-ins, to intercede for the church. Give them specific prayer assignments each week—and be sure to brag to the rest of the church about their faithfulness in this prayer ministry!

[2]See www.syatp.com.
[3]See www.momsintouch.org.

Prayer hot line—Establish a phone line to receive prayer concerns from the church and community. Ideally, callers will have opportunity to speak to a live person who will pray with them. Answering machines work as well, as long as you faithfully follow up with those who call. Be sure they know that you received the call and are praying as you promised to do.

Noonday prayer meetings—Using a model that produced a great revival around the world in 1857–58, establish prayer meetings during the lunch hour. Encourage members either to join you at your church for prayer or to establish prayer meetings in their own workplaces. Pray particularly for God to send a revival to your community.

Fathers Focus on Prayer (FFP) group—Call the men of your church to prayer by establishing an FFP group that meets monthly to pray for their families. This group may work alongside another men's organization (such as Promise Keepers), but make sure that prayer remains the focus.

Pew praying—Enlist a team of prayer warriors to meet at the church and pray over each pew prior to the worship services.

Missionary birthday praying—Get a list of birthdays of the missionaries your church supports, and pray for the missionaries on that day. If permissible, send a prayer/birthday card.

Prayer library—Develop a church library section that includes several resources on prayer. See the resource list in appendix 7 for help in beginning your collection.

Prayer offerings—In the same way that the church sets aside time to give a financial offering, plan a prayer offering time in the worship service. Guide members to focus on God and to pray for specific current concerns each week.

CONCLUSION . . . AND GETTING STARTED

So are you ready to lead your church toward being a prayer-driven church? If you are, remember these fundamental principles for increasing the prayer ministry in your congregation:

Don't Be Afraid to Start Small

It may take a while to produce a large number of prayer warriors in your church. Be patient. Get one more person involved at a time. I'd much rather have a handful of committed warriors than hundreds of people who just *say* they're committed to prayer.

Don't Give Up Easily

Satan doesn't want your prayer ministry to be effective, so he'll fire darts of discouragement at you. Take up the shield of faith (Ephesians 6:16), and stand firm in your commitment to be prayer-driven.

Do Pray

This probably sounds like a strange principle, doesn't it? But when we so emphasize prayer, our talking to one another *about* prayer can often replace our talking to God *in* prayer. Don't let that happen!

At the time of this writing, my wife and I are about three months away from moving into a new home. Just last week, the electricians ran the wiring throughout the framing of the house. Potential power now resides in the walls, except that the electricity hasn't been fully connected yet. Disconnected power still leaves us in the dark at night.

That's the situation I see in many churches today. The power of God evidenced through prayer is available to us, but somehow most churches aren't fully connected yet. Prayer power remains only potential power for too many churches.

My hope is that this little book will help you and your church become more fully connected to the power of prayer. May God bless you as you work toward becoming a praying church.

QUESTIONS FOR REFLECTION AND DISCUSSION

1. Which of the prayer methods listed in this chapter could be most quickly and effectively applied in your church?

2. Which of these methods most captures *your* attention—that is, which one might God be asking *you* to do?

3. Now that you've completed this study, what obstacles to becoming a prayer-driven church do you see in your congregation? Pray together with your group that God will remove those barriers.

4. What is *your* first step toward helping your church become a praying church?

5. With your group, determine what your follow-up to this study will be. Will some group members lead others through this study? How will you hold each other accountable to a new vision for prayer?

APPENDIX 1

Personal Prayer Survey

Using the scale below, determine your level of agreement or disagreement with each of the following statements.

1	2	3	4	5
Strongly disagree	Disagree	Uncertain	Agree	Strongly agree

_____ 1. I pray every day.

_____ 2. I believe that prayer works—that God hears me and responds when I pray.

_____ 3. Sometimes I'm not very consistent in prayer.

_____ 4. I want someone to teach me more about how to pray.

_____ 5. I want to believe that prayer is effective, but sometimes I struggle to believe it.

_____ 6. I would attend if our church offered a training course on prayer.

_____ 7. I pray more when I'm facing difficulty than I do when things are going well.

_____ 8. I pray at least once a week for the salvation of someone who is not a Christian.

_____ 9. I pray at least once a week for my pastor and church staff members.

_____ 10. I'm not sure that my prayers make much difference.

_____ 11. Someone has specifically taught me how to pray.

_____ 12. I pray at least once a week for our government
officials.

_____ 13. I have a personal prayer partner who holds me
accountable for praying.

_____ 14. I would like my church leaders to teach more
about prayer.

_____ 15. Sometimes my prayer life becomes routine, so I'd
like to learn about more methods for praying.

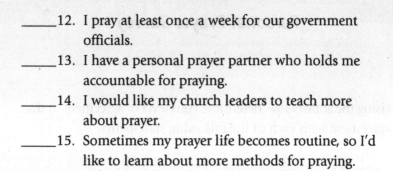

APPENDIX 2

Budget Worksheet

ANNUAL BUDGET—PRAYER MINISTRY

Salary or stipend for prayer leader
(if not a volunteer position) . . . .

Salary for secretarial support
(if not volunteer) . . . .

Newsletter costs . . . .

Mailing costs (publicity,
prayer cards, etc.) . . . .

Training events . . . .

Costs for speakers
   Honorarium and travel
   Advertising costs
   Resources and supplies

    Costs for speakers subtotal . . . .

Prayer line telephone costs . . . .

Costs for furnishing a prayer room
    Furniture (desk, chair, lamp) _____
    Card files and supplies   _____
    Maps   _____
    CD or tape player + music   _____
    Computer/Internet access   _____
    Forms   _____

        Costs for furnishing a
        prayer room subtotal . . . . [_____]

Costs for other resources
        (books, audiotapes, videotapes) . . . . . . [_____]

Costs for fellowships, meals
    Annual banquet to
      recognize volunteers   _____
    Prayer breakfasts   _____
    Refreshments for
      training events   _____
    Leader's prayer
      partners events   _____

    Costs for fellowships, meals subtotal . . . . [_____]

Conference expenses (to provide
    training for leaders) . . . . [_____]

Miscellaneous expenses . . . . [_____]

TOTAL: . . . . [_____]

Prayer Room Layout

THE INTERCESSORY PRAYER ROOM
Ash Street Baptist Church
Forest Park, Georgia

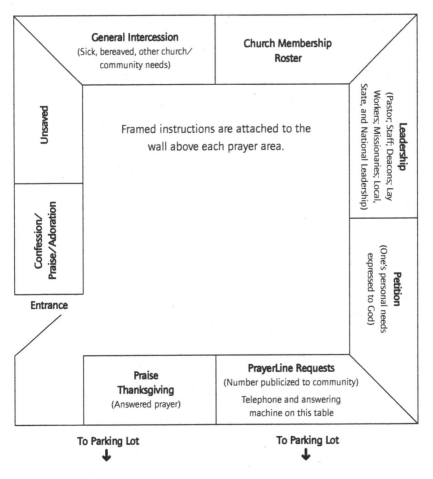

General Intercession
(Sick, bereaved, other church/
community needs)

Church Membership
Roster

Unsaved

Leadership
(Pastor; Staff; Deacons; Lay
Workers; Missionaries; Local,
State, and National Leadership)

Framed instructions are attached to the
wall above each prayer area.

Confession/
Praise/Adoration

Petition
(One's personal needs
expressed to God)

Entrance

Praise
Thanksgiving
(Answered prayer)

PrayerLine Requests
(Number publicized to community)

Telephone and answering
machine on this table

To Parking Lot
↓

To Parking Lot
↓

APPENDIX 4

Prayer Request Card

Please place this completed form in the offering plate or in a prayer request box, or bring it to the intercessory prayer room.

Please pray for: _____

Address: _____

City: _____ State: _____ Zip: _____

Phone: _____ E-mail address:_____

Prayer concern: _____

_____

_____

_____

Would this person like to receive
   a prayer card? ___ Yes ___ No ___ Uncertain

Is this person a Christian? ___ Yes ___ No ___ Uncertain

Is this person a member
   of our church? ___ Yes ___ No ___ Uncertain

Person making request: _____

Phone: _____ E-mail address:_____

- -

For Prayer Room Use Only

Submitted to the prayer room leaders: _____

Prayer card sent:_____

Recorded in prayer station:_____

Follow-up contact:_____

APPENDIX 5

Our Strategy for Multiplying Pray-ers

Use this form to plan your strategy for multiplying prayer warriors in your church. List any activities, training sessions, or events that will help you reach your goals.

Expectations	Teaching
Plan: _____ _____ _____ Date: _____	Plan: _____ _____ _____ Date: _____
Plan: _____ _____ _____ Date: _____	Plan: _____ _____ _____ Date: _____
Plan: _____ _____ _____ Date: _____	Plan: _____ _____ _____ Date: _____
Plan: _____ _____ _____ Date: _____	Plan: _____ _____ _____ Date: _____
Plan: _____ _____ _____ Date: _____	Plan: _____ _____ _____ Date: _____

(continued on the following page)

Relationships	Involvement
Plan: _____ _____ _____ Date: _____	Plan: _____ _____ _____ Date: _____
Plan: _____ _____ _____ Date: _____	Plan: _____ _____ _____ Date: _____
Plan: _____ _____ _____ Date: _____	Plan: _____ _____ _____ Date: _____
Plan: _____ _____ _____ Date: _____	Plan: _____ _____ _____ Date: _____
Plan: _____ _____ _____ Date: _____	Plan: _____ _____ _____ Date: _____

APPENDIX 6

Prayer Chain Guidelines

1. The purpose of the prayer chain is to pray for emergency and daily spiritual, physical, and material needs of the friends, families, and members of _____ Church.

2. Incoming prayer requests should be forwarded to the prayer chain captain, _____, at phone # _____, who will then start the chain.

3. When you receive the request, write it down *word for word* in your prayer notebook. **Repeat** the request to your caller to verify your recorded information. Do not discuss other issues during the phone call.

4. Immediately call the next person on your prayer chain list. If there is no answer, continue calling down the list until a prayer chain member answers. The last person on the chain should *always* call the captain to verify that the requests have been properly received.

5. Immediately after making the call, pray for the requests.

6. Notify the prayer chain captain when you hear of answers to prayer. The captain will forward the information to prayer chain members. Be sure to thank God for answered prayers.

7. If at any point you cannot effectively fulfill your obligations as a prayer chain member, please inform the prayer chain captain.

Prayer Chain Covenant with God: "Father, I promise I will fervently pray about each request I receive, and I will trust you to answer in your own time and in accordance with your perfect will."

Signed: _____

Date: _____

APPENDIX 7

Suggested Resources

Aldrich, Joe. *Prayer Summits: Seeking God's Agenda for Your Community*. Portland, Ore.: Multnomah, 1992.

Bryant, David. *Concerts of Prayer*. Ventura, Calif.: Regal, 1988.

Cymbala, Jim, *Fresh Wind, Fresh Fire*. Grand Rapids: Zondervan, 1997.

Dennis, Jay, with Marilyn Jeffcoat. *The Prayer Experiment: Discovering a Prayer That Could Change Your World*. Grand Rapids: Zondervan, 2001.

Dunnam, Maxie. *The Workbook of Living Prayer*. Nashville: Upper Room, 1994.

Franklin, John, compiler. *A House of Prayer: Prayer Ministries in Your Church*. Nashville: Lifeway, 1999.

Frizzell, Gregory R. *Biblical Patterns for Powerful Church Prayer Meetings*. Memphis, Tenn.: Master Design, 1999.

Graf, Jonathan L., and Lani C. Hinkle, eds. *My House Shall Be a House of Prayer*. Colorado Springs: Pray!Books, 2001.

Griffith, Jill. *How to Have a Dynamic Church Prayer Ministry*. Colorado Springs: Wagner Publications, 1999.

Hawthorne, Steve, and Graham Kendrick. *Prayerwalking: Praying On-Site with Insight*. Lake Mary, Fla.: Creation House, 1993.

Helms, Elaine. *If My People ... Pray: Steps to Effective Church Prayer Ministry*. Marietta, Ga.: Church Prayer Ministries, 2000.

Kamstra, Douglas A. *The Praying Church Idea Book*. Grand Rapids: Faith Alive Christian Resources, 2001.

Martin, Glen, and Dian Ginter. *Power House: A Step-by-Step Guide to Building a Church That Prays*. Nashville: Broadman & Holman, 1994.

Pedersen, Bjorn. *Face to Face with God in Your Church: Establishing a Prayer Ministry*. Minneapolis: Augsburg Fortress, 1995.

Piper, John. *A Hunger for God: Desiring God through Fasting and Prayer*. Wheaton, Ill.: Crossway, 1997.

Sheets, Dutch. *How to Pray for Lost Loved Ones*. Ventura, Calif.: Regal, 2001.

Shelley, Marshall, ed. *Deepening Your Ministry through Prayer and Personal Growth*. Nashville: Moorings, 1996.

Spurgeon, Charles. *Only a Prayer Meeting: Studies on Prayer Meetings and Prayer Meeting Addresses*. Great Britain: Christian Focus, 2000.

Teykl, Terry. *Acts 29: Blueprint for the House of Prayer*. Muncie, Ind.: Prayer Point Press, 1997.

_____. *Making Room to Pray: How to Start and Maintain a Prayer Room in Your Church*. Anderson, Ind.: Bristol Books, 1993.

_____. *Prayer Room Intercessor's Handbook*. Muncie, Ind.: Prayer Point Press, 1999.

_____. *Preyed On or Prayed For*. Muncie, Ind.: Prayer Point Press, 2000.

Vander Griend, Alvin, with Edith Bajema. *The Praying Church Sourcebook*. Grand Rapids: Church Development Resources, 1997.

Wagner, C. Peter. *Churches That Pray*. Ventura, Calif.: Regal, 1997.

_____. *Prayer Shield*. Ventura, Calif.: Regal, 1992.

ZONDERVAN PRACTICAL MINISTRY GUIDES
Paul E. Engle, Series Editor

SERVING AS A CHURCH GREETER
This practical guidebook will help you reach out to people who need to experience the warmth of belonging to a church family. **Softcover (ISBN 0-310-24764-0).**

SERVING AS A CHURCH USHER
Your impact as an usher is enormous both in meeting the needs of people and in keeping the church service running smoothly. **Softcover (ISBN 0-310-24763-2).**

SERVING IN YOUR CHURCH MUSIC MINISTRY
This wise, concise guidebook will help you harness your God-given musical talent as a gift to the body of Christ. **Softcover (ISBN 0-310-24101-4).**

SERVING BY SAFEGUARDING YOUR CHURCH
Church ought to be the safest place on earth. Here's how to fulfill that goal in practical ways, Includes diagrams, checklists, and resources lists. **Softcover (ISBN 0-310-24105-7).**

SERVING IN CHURCH VISITATION
Whether visiting people in their homes, in the hospital, or in a restaurant over a cup of coffee, the simple act of connecting with others is filled with powerful possibilities. **Softcover (ISBN 0-310-24103-0).**

SERVING IN YOUR CHURCH PRAYER MINISTRY
God moves in praying churches in ways that planning and programs alone can't produce. **Softcover (ISBN 0-310-24758-6).**

SERVING IN YOUR CHURCH NURSERY
Whether you're leading your church's nursery ministry, serving in it, or just thinking of getting involved, you will welcome the expert insights, encouragement, and resources this book offers. **Softcover (ISBN 0-310-24104-9).**

Pick up your copies today at your favorite bookstore!

GRAND RAPIDS, MICHIGAN 49530 USA

WWW.ZONDERVAN.COM

We want to hear from you. Please send your comments about this
book to us in care of zreview@zondervan.com. Thank you.

GRAND RAPIDS, MICHIGAN 49530 USA

WWW.ZONDERVAN.COM